SISTER POWER

SISTER POWER

How Phenomenal Black Women Are Rising to the Top

Patricia Reid-Merritt, D.S.W.

John Wiley & Sons, Inc.
New York • Chichester • Brisbane • Toronto • Singapore

This text is printed on acid-free paper.

Published by John Wiley & Sons, Inc.

Library of Congress Cataloging-in-Publication Data

Reid-Merritt, Patricia.
Sister power : how phenomenal black women are rising to the top / Patricia Reid-Merritt.
p. cm.
Includes index.
ISBN 0-471-10461-2 (alk. paper)
1. Afro-American women. 2. Afro-American leadership. I. Title.
E185.86.R416 1997 96-4208
305.48'896073—dc20

Printed in the United States of America
10 9 8 7 6 5 4 3 2 1

To my sisters,
Darlene, Jessica, Marie, *and* Suzette,
To my sister aunt, Nita,
and to my mother,
Etrulia Lucille,
who taught me everything I ever needed to know
about being a powerful black woman

I'm a woman
Phenomenally.
Phenomenal woman.
That's me.

—*Maya Angelou*
1978

Contents

Preface

In the early spring of 1986, I was in New York to attend a celebration sponsored by the Association of Black Women in Higher Education. It was being held at the Metropolitan Museum's Temple of Dendur to honor the nation's black female college and university presidents, among them Dr. Reatha Clark King and Dr. Vera King Farris. Joining them in this grand event was a sparkling array of sisters, including Dr. Dolores Cross, a member of Governor Cuomo's cabinet; Dr. Gwendolyn Calvert Baker, executive director of the YWCA of USA; Shirley Dennis, director of U.S. Department of Labor Women's Bureau; Susan L. Taylor, editor in chief of *Essence* magazine; Faye Wattleton, president of Planned Parenthood Federation of America; as well as other sisters who were judges, commissioners, and CEOs, along with their equally powerful black male counterparts. An aura of confidence, joy, victory, serenity, and sisterhood filtered through the air. I had never seen so many powerful black women in one place. I felt overwhelmed by their humility and simply blessed to be in their presence.

When I reflect on my own past, it is clear to me why I have always felt so strongly about the need for competent, committed leadership from the African American sisterhood. I was born into a two-parent, working-class family in urban West Philadelphia in the fifties; within a few years we—my mother, myself, and eight sisters and brothers—had slipped into a single-parent welfare-class family. I was surrounded by many positive images of black women as mothers, wives, and lovers; religious women and scandalous women; workers, nurturers, sufferers, and survivors. In all of these multifaceted roles, nowhere but nowhere did I see images of sisters with power or influence. The only black woman I knew who wasn't a factory worker or a domestic was my fifth-grade teacher, Mrs. Jeffries. I remember her well because she insisted that we capitalize the *N* in Negro. "Never strive to be a little *n*," she would say. "I want you all to grow up to be a big *N*." And I knew I wanted to be a big *N*, but I never fully anticipated all that might be involved in that process.

I was not quite a teenager when the nation celebrated the 100th anniversary of the Emancipation Proclamation, an event that galvanized the developing protest movement in the black community. I came of age in an era of "firsts," as the struggles of the Civil Rights and women's movements began to open up new opportunities everywhere. In the seventies and eighties scores of first-time achievements for blacks and women unfolded in the public and private sectors. Barbara Jordan and Yvonne Brathwaite Burke had joined Shirley Chisholm in Congress, and Patricia Roberts Harris joined President Carter's cabinet. Black women also started to move up the corporate ladder. It was a startling phenomenon by any measure.

In New York, Massachusetts, Pennsylvania, New Jersey, and Arkansas, black women joined the governors' cabinets. The National Education Association, one of the nation's most powerful unions, elected Mary Hatwood Futrell as its president. Dr. Dorothy Harris assumed the presidency of the National Association of Social Workers, a professional and advocacy body that almost single-handedly is responsible for shaping the government's massive aid program to senior citizens. Black women were running two of the nation's largest urban school districts—Dr. Constance Clayton in Philadelphia and Dr. Floretta McKenzie in Washington, D.C. By the end of the eighties, Oprah Winfrey had become one of the most successful women in the entertainment industry.

All of a sudden, there weren't three black female college presidents, there were thirty-three. Drs. Niara Sudarkasa, Jewel Plummer Cobb, Marguerite Ross Barnett, Reatha Clark King, and Vera King Farris became university presidents, each one marking the first time a black woman had assumed that position in their respective institutions. Dr. Johnnetta B. Cole was named president of Spelman College in 1987, the first time that a black woman was entrusted with the presidency of this historic black college for women. And in 1989, Sharon Pratt Kelly became mayor of Washington, D.C.

The nineties brought more news of black women leaping into positions of power. In 1992 Hazel O'Leary and Dr. Joycelyn Elders joined President Bill Clinton's cabinet, and Carol Moseley-Braun (D-Ill.) became the first black woman elected to the Senate. An explosion of nine black women from seven different states were sent to the House of Representatives as part of the 103rd Congress. In 1993, Ann M. Fudge's career became the black female corporate success story when she was named president of Maxwell House Coffee Company. In 1995, Ruth Simmons assumed the presidency of Smith College, one of the nation's most elite women's colleges.

My own rapid rise out of poverty had been confounding. I was among the first of eleven students who integrated Cabrini, an all-white, Catholic girls college, the first to benefit from a fellowship program at Temple University's new School of Social Administration, and the first black female to receive tenure and promotion at Richard Stockton College, in Pomona, New Jersey.

The four local newspapers serving my suburban area were always there to chronicle my progress, and the community's expectations were running high. I tried to do it all. I engaged in community and professional activism and emerged as president, chairwoman, director, and had other titles that designated me as the leader. I received both cheers and jeers for my increasing visibility and influence. I was never certain if the rewards were greater than the punishments. Various agendas were hidden around me like explosives in a minefield. At times, people seemed downright hostile for no apparent reason. By 1987, the year I turned thirty-six, I was confused: What was this black female leadership thing all about?

I soon discovered that my experiences and concerns were not unique; other sisters were raising similar questions. Was our experience the norm? What could we expect if we continued on the road to power? What could we expect if we quit?

Attending that historic party in New York recharged my spirits and fueled my curiosity about black female leadership. These sisters seemed mythic characters, larger than life. Seeing them in person made me feel that to be a successful leader I needed to be doing what they were doing. But how had they done it?

Given the obstacles that exist for every black woman in America, sisters so visible at the top of the American power ladder must be exceptional. And yet we know almost nothing about them. We know little about how they live their lives, what they stand for as a group, or whether they are moving specific ideas in a specific direction. To understand the nature of black female leadership I wanted to find answers to fundamental questions:

Where did these influential women come from? How did they reach their positions? How are they using their power, and what can African Americans and white folks expect from them? Do they really hold power in their hands? Or is their power a temporary illusion?

I set out on a mission to seek out and to discuss with them the impact of the power and leadership experience on black women. The unlikely coupling of sisters and power is the focus of this book.

All of the women who participated in this book did so because they are eager to share with other Americans their vision of leadership. Above all, they want younger women, particularly young sisters, to know that they are ready to encourage and guide them. These sisters have arrived, and they intend to bring others along with them. They are united in this goal: Though they may have been the first, they don't want to be the last.

This is an attempt to harness the knowledge and wisdom of sisters who have traveled once-forbidden roads. Herein begins the story of their wants and desires, successes and failures, their plans for social change, and their visions for a new style of leadership. Their hope and mine is that *Sister Power* will help prepare and guide a new generation of black women struggle to take control of their own destinies.

Acknowledgments

Over the past nine years, I've learned what every writer knows to be the fundamental truth in the authorship of any new product: What started with a burst of creativity proved to be a long, arduous process. All of my family and friends, acquaintances, and sometimes even casual bystanders knew that I was struggling to complete this work. Their names are too numerous to mention, but I thank them all for the support and encouragement they gave me over the years.

Particular appreciation goes to Richard Stockton College and its president, Dr. Vera King Farris. Stockton awarded me a Distinguished Fellowship grant, which provided the seed money to begin the study, and on more than one occasion provided additional finances and resources to help complete the book.

The forty-five women who allowed me to conduct in-depth interviews and shared their personal experiences are the primary contriabutors. Without their generosity this book would not exist. Space would not permit everyone's story to be included, but in the end all of their contributions played an important part in the overall content, and I am deeply indebted to them.

Literary agents, Barbara Lowenstein and Madeleine Morel "discovered me" after hearing about the study from Linda Villarosa. They were a constant source of support throughout the project.

My heartfelt thanks to Josleen Wilson, who worked with me day and night on the manuscript. Josleen's writing skills and technical expertise guided this book from proposal to its full completion. As a novice writer, I was often uncertain as to which approach would best present the massive amounts of material to be included in the book. Josleen worked it all out.

Editor Hana Lane was a pleasure to work with, contradicting every negative story I ever heard about publishing. My special thanks to Carole Hall, the associate publisher, who believed in the project from the very beginning and offered insight and advice at every stage of its development.

My thanks to all of my sister friends who helped with the research, contacted powerful black women, and continued to encourage me throughout this long journey: Dr. Bernadette Penceal, Dr. Patricia Carey, Charlotte Thomas-Hawkins, Dr. Sonia Gonsalves, Earnestine Simpson Steverson, Kylthia Roberts, Sharon Ingram, Kimberly Rusunungyko, Shirley Bookhart, Wanola Thomas, Carolyn Lurry-Mapp, Nitchell Perkins, and Jan Douglass. The hard work and dedication to excellence of all the young sisters at Afro-One Dance, Drama and Drum Theatre, Inc., fueled my spirit. They embody the hopes and dreams of previous generations, and I know their contributions to the advancement of the sisterhood will be great. And thanks to the men of Afro-One, who continue to inspire me with the beat of the drums.

Getting through the gatekeepers was often a difficult task. Many played a pivotal role in helping me to conduct the interviews. A special thanks to the administrative assistants, secretaries, receptionists, special assistants to, office staff, and other personnel for getting me through the front door. The moments when I felt most disheartened about ever obtaining an interview, they came through with words of encouragement and an appointment time. And I am deeply indebted to former Congressman Walter E. Fauntroy who provided a letter of endorsement at the very beginning of this project.

A very special thanks to Dr. Paul Lyons and Dr. Sherman Labovitz, who, without hesitation, offered a male perspective on certain issues and helped to clarify many of the theoretical concepts that I struggled with. And to my closest friends, colleagues, and brothers in the struggle, Dr. Thaddeus P. Mathis and Dr. Curtis Leonard, who have served as mentors, confidants, and intellectual sparring partners for the past twenty years.

Transcribing the tapes was an enormous undertaking accomplished by the skillful work and contributions of Gwen Jones and Joyce Dipoltio. I am also grateful to those who reviewed early drafts of the manuscript and helped to shape its direction: Dr. Molefi Kete Asante, Joanne Grant, Kathryn D. Leary, Dr. Julianne Malveaux, Dr. Miriam Monges, Alexis Moore, Dr. Linda Nelson, and Dr. Jackie Pope. Their comments and insights were extremely helpful.

My stepson, Gregory Merritt, put me in cyberspace and came to my rescue whenever the computer assumed a position of intellectual superiority. I love you dearly.

My thanks and love to my daughter, Christina Bookhart, who served as in-house editor, researcher, typist, and sounding board; to my son, Brahim Bookhart, who always inquired, with great sensitivity and compassion, about the length of time it was taking me to complete the book; and to my husband, Bill, who was always there for me. Your love and support are everything to me.

1

Inspiration

> I have discovered a lot about this business of calling black women aggressive. It's the "hands on your hips" kind of thing. The "in your face" kind of thing. We were not socialized in the niceties of diplomacy. Everything we hear, from when we start to go to Sunday school, is tell the truth, speak up, say what's on your mind. This is what I was taught. This is what everybody in my neighborhood did. This is not something I plotted or strategized. This is where I come from. This is who I am.
>
> —*Congresswoman Maxine Waters (D-Calif.)*

July 29, 1994, in Washington, D.C., started out just like any other hot and humid summer day in the nation's capital. About a hundred tourists were milling up and down the steps of the Capitol, taking in the sights. On the top tier of steps, less than 100 feet from the front door, someone had set up a life-size plaster statue of Jesus Christ painted in bright colors. Next to the statue, a woman with a loudspeaker extolled all sinners to prepare for the Second Coming. On the other side of Jesus sat a homeless man, sweating in a long-sleeved jacket, holding up a poster:

> I LOST MY HEALTH IN WWII. I HAVE A BAD HEART AND HIGH BLOOD PRESSURE AND GOUT. GOT NO MORE LIFE. I CANNOT GET MY GI RIGHTS OR SS OR FOOD STAMPS. CAN'T GET NO MORE HELP FROM THE U.S.A. BECAUSE I'M ONE OF THE BLACK DOG SLAVES OF THE U.S.A. AND A NIGER IN 1994.

The man was so dirty and sun scorched that it was impossible to tell if he was black or white. Either way, he was only one of thousands of homeless people residing somewhere in the nation's capital. He had simply taken his case a little closer to the head office. In most ways the scene was politics as usual, but this day held a surprise.

The night before, in room 2128 of the Rayburn House Office Building, a bipartisan committee on banking, finance and urban affairs had started the Whitewater hearings to investigate the failed Arkansas banking and land deal in which President and Mrs. Clinton had invested. House Republicans were hoping to turn the hearings into a full-scale political soap opera comparable to Watergate.

C-SPAN was duly present, and the cameras were rolling when Congressman Peter King (R-N.Y.) called Mrs. Clinton's executive assistant, Margaret Williams, a sister, as his first witness.

King opened up with a series of sharp questions aimed to humiliate the witness. When Williams denied having received a memo concerning the First Lady's finances and denied having made certain negative comments about her boss's reactions to the investigation, King accused her of lying.

Williams answered, "Mr. King, my honesty in this matter does not depend on whether or not you believe me."

King continued hammering away at the same questions, and with every repeated answer accused Williams of lying.

Henry B. Gonzalez (D-Tex.), chairman of the proceedings, finally interrupted and told King to stop badgering the witness. King didn't stop. Suddenly Congresswoman Maxine Waters, the second-term Democrat from California's Twenty-ninth District and one of fifty-five committee members, interjected: "Mr. Chairman, the gentleman is out of order."

"I have the right to ask questions," King retorted. "You had your chance. Why don't you just sit there."

"You are out of order," Waters said.

"You're always out of order!" King answered.

Waters: Shut up!

King: What was the last remark?

Waters: You heard what I said.

King: I didn't hear. I'd like to hear again. I would like you to say it again.

Waters: I said, "You're out of order."

King: Okay. I said, "You're always out of order."

Gonzalez tried to silence them, to little avail.

King: Could I speak for myself? I just—

Waters: He is out of order, Mr. Chairman.

King: I don't think anyone needs . . .

Waters: Order, Mr. Chairman.

King: . . . Ms. Waters butting in all the time. Nobody cares about you!

Gonzalez again chastised King for his treatment of the witness. But King's attention could not be diverted from Maxine Waters.

"My only outburst, if it was one," he said, "was at Ms. Waters, not at Ms. Williams or any members of this panel."

Surprisingly, Waters did not reply, and Gonzalez moved the proceedings on to the next witness. He didn't seem to realize that the shouting had just begun.

The next morning, which was Friday, July 29, in a speech before the full House of Representatives, King launched a direct attack on Waters: "Her remarks, even for the gentlelady from California, went to a new low. She's not going to tell me to shut up. She's not going to tell the American people to shut up. And I'm not going to stop until we get to the root of Whitewater!"

Anyone who knew Waters at all, knew she would never let him get away with it. However, instead of taking King's insults personally, Waters lined herself up in defense of Margaret Williams and all the other women in America. "I'm pleased I was able to come to her defense," she responded on the House floor. "The day is over when men can intimidate and badger women." Waters continued speaking, even as Republican representatives began shouting her down.

The lawmaker in the chair that day, Congresswoman Carrie P. Meek (D-Fla.), another sister, began to gavel Waters to stop. "The gentlelady from California, you must suspend." But Waters refused to surrender the microphone.

Up and down the halls of Congress everyone was talking about the verbal brawl taking place on the House floor. "They've never seen nothing like this before," one black woman said. A young white man was next, saying in awe, "Nobody better put their hands on Congresswoman Waters." A hastily gathered chorus of sisters cheered in the halls of Congress, "It's a new day."

Back on the House floor, Republican representatives were demanding that Waters be forcibly removed from the podium. As the sergeant at arms approached the podium, Waters turned on her heel and walked out.

The Speaker of the House, Thomas Foley, tried to regain order. He castigated Waters for "conduct unbecoming a member of the House," although he added that her *words* were not out of order. He ruled she would not be allowed to speak for the rest of the day.

Congresswoman Patricia Schroeder (D-Colo.) immediately defended her congressional sister, claiming that shouting from the House floor may have prevented Waters from hearing Carrie Meek's request to suspend.

Word of political insurrection spreads like wildfire on the Hill. Kweisi Mfume (D-Md.), head of the Congressional Black Caucus, hurriedly left an emergency meeting on Haiti and dashed to the House floor. Mfume, a grassroots, street-smart homeboy from Baltimore's Thirty-third District, now the newly appointed national director of the NAACP, wasn't about to sit still for any attack on a caucus member. But it was all over by the time he made it onto the House floor. Foley had already asked for, and received, unanimous consent to restore Waters's speaking privileges.

The next day, reaction set in. Conservatives had a field day joking with viewers who called into media talk shows to complain about the uppity black congresswoman's inappropriate behavior.

By day three, white Republican women had begun making speeches on the House floor in defense of Representative King. That night, CNN reported, "The first lesson of Whitewater may very well be that political blood is thicker than sisterhood." Indeed, though there may be mutual issues that bond white and black women, on this particular day the fight for respect didn't appear to be one of them.

Nevertheless, Maxine's strong public statement delivered a clear message to the power elite: White congressmen could expect the new wave of congressional black women to be listening to and watching their investigations, voting on their bills, and presenting bills of their own. And during that process they expected to be treated as equals and with respect. She also made something else clear: When you're a sister with power, at times forthright aggressiveness is the only language powerful men understand. Sometimes you just have to kick ass in public arenas.

Maxine Waters epitomizes Sister Power, a unique combination of historical legacy, a sense of social justice, hard work, and style. There are variations among powerful black women, but she's as representative as they come. At the same time, her story, like theirs, is unique. A perusal of Waters's early life would not immediately suggest that she was destined for leadership. Maxine Waters was born in St. Louis in 1938, a time when the decade-long Depression had already eroded the spirit and flesh of America's poor. Maxine was the fifth child of her very attractive mother, Velma (Moore) Carr, and a father whom she never knew well. Her parents separated when she was two years old.

After Maxine's birth, Velma had eight more children. As in poor families everywhere, long-range plans by necessity gave way to day-to-day needs. "People in these circumstances can't see very far ahead," Maxine said. "People are just happy to survive, happy to get up the next morning and find some food to eat." Maxine described her mother as an uneducated woman, but strong, with a keen instinct for survival.

While the family struggled, the nation itself began to experience an economic revival. During World War II everything, and everyone, seemed to be on the move. With so much flux, change seemed inevitable, but the Midwest and Southwest had been hammered nearly to depletion by the Depression, and little movement was felt inside the stagnating poverty of St. Louis's black neighborhoods.

Maxine's earliest memories are of women in the neighborhood who helped care for her and her siblings. "Back in those days, we didn't have child care that we could afford," she said. "Poor people didn't. Somebody kept your children, usually older women in the neighborhood. And it was through them that young women learned everything. If you came home and found your child ill with a fever, they told you what to do. 'Take this child home and do this, do that, give them this and do that.'

"They were more than baby-sitters. They were like grandmothers. They would tell you how to fix a meal. If you complained that you didn't have the money and that food was short, they would say, 'Well, honey, you have to learn how to make a meal. If you take this cornmeal and add some hot water, you will have corn bread. Then you could add this and that. . . .' Then they would tell you how to shop at the Goodwill to buy clothes."

Maxine remembers herself as a skinny, dark-skinned little girl, constantly competing for the family spotlight, an uphill road given the number of children in the household. She was also the first dark child born in her family, and her three older sisters never let her live it down.

Older black women in the community always encouraged her, particularly her teachers, who singled her out for extra attention. "I had wonderful teachers in elementary school—teachers whose homes I went to, who let me stay with them after school and play the piano, mess around with it until I learned to play a little. They encouraged me to do things, they made sure that I was included in all kinds of activities. They saw life clearly. The way they related to children and the kind of support I received from them was extremely important. They knew what they could do for children, and they were firm in their beliefs."

Throughout Maxine's childhood older black women continued to play this teaching role and gave her palpable evidence that she was special. The picture one gets of Maxine as a child is of a bright little girl trying to develop her talents and make herself recognized.

Churchgoing added structure to Maxine's life. "We spent a lot of time attending Sunday school, the BPU [Baptist Peoples Union] and the eleven o'clock service. Just like the book *All I Really Need to Know I Learned in Kindergarten*, everything I learned, I learned in church: respect for other human beings, no lying, cheating, or stealing. I think the Ten Commandments will serve most people well over their lifetime."

Nationwide, when World War II ended, a period of calm and prosperity followed. However, running parallel to the peace was the menace of the Cold War. The global threat of the atom and hydrogen bombs fueled America's fear of communism, leading to abuse of individual and civil rights during the McCarthy era. One of the nation's worries was that black Americans would be especially vulnerable to Communist propaganda because their freedom and rights had never been secured. During the paradoxical fifties, the modern Civil Rights movement was born.

Against this shifting domestic panorama, Waters came of age. "I knew something wasn't right after I graduated from high school and started looking for a job," she said. "I went to the gas company and the phone company and the major department stores. Strangely enough, nobody in those offices looked like me. I kept calling. I went back to the gas company and applied for a job, and back to the phone company and applied for a job. I went day in and day out. And still, it did not dawn on me that I was not getting those jobs because I was black. I didn't quite get it.

"I ended up working in a garment factory. That's where all young black girls worked at the time. I finally realized that there were jobs for blacks and jobs for whites. Even in the factory, black girls got the worst jobs. You couldn't be a cutter, couldn't be a presser, you couldn't be anything. From that point on, I began to understand racism and discrimination."

On the surface, Maxine appeared to adjust to her designated lot in life. She married a young man named Edward Waters, and by 1960, she had given birth to two children, Edward Jr. and Karen. "Even when I was a young married woman, it was the older women in the community who helped me with my children, who fixed soup for me, so that when I came home from work at night there was some hot food."

Her most valuable lesson, she said, was learning to listen closely when older women spoke. Through them, she was able to sustain her own sense of self. "They shared with you their knowledge and their experience and were happy to do it. That's one thing older black women loved to do, and that was to tell you what to do."

The job situation for black people in St. Louis was probably no better or worse than in any other part of the country. However, everyone dreamed about the golden land on the other side of the mountains. When their circumstances didn't improve, Maxine and Edward decided to make the move to California. They arrived in Los Angeles, and settled in the Watts section of the city. The golden land didn't pan out the way they had hoped. Opportunity proved to be just as scarce as it had been in St. Louis. Their hopes fading, Maxine took a low-paying job in a downtown garment factory, and Edward found a menial job in a printing plant. Maxine kept looking for a better position and eventually landed a job as an operator for Pacific Telephone. She was forced to quit when she had a miscarriage that led to medical complications.

Unknown to her, other forces were at work that would change her destiny. In the midsixties Maxine heard about Head Start, one of several federally funded programs initiated by Lyndon Johnson as part of the War on Poverty. She applied and was accepted for an internship as an assistant teacher. At Head Start she first met the grassroots activists who eventually opened up a brand-new vista for her and many others. "I remember the names of these women very well. There was Mary Henry, who still runs the Avalon Community Center. Early on she organized a program under an umbrella agency called the Economic and Youth Opportunities Agency (EYOA). She was a spokesperson for the entire community, and you could always see her in the neighborhood and in local media.

"Another woman named Opal Jones ran a program called the Neighborhood Adult Participation Project. Prior to the War on Poverty, most of these women had never had any opportunity for leadership. We didn't have the professionals, the doctors or lawyers. But these weren't those kind of women anyway. These were activist women. These were women who created new ways of doing things."

She described her experiences at Head Start as initiating a profound period of self-discovery that she stumbled into as if by the grace of God. "We were taught to teach the children self-esteem through the activities we did within the classroom. In the process, we learned an awful lot about ourselves, too. We had encounter groups and I started to listen to other people, and to listen to myself, and to raise questions of myself. To come to grips with what I liked and what I did not like, who I liked and who I did not like. I learned not to be afraid. I learned to express myself and act on my beliefs. And that's when I began to take power for myself."

In some ways, Head Start was a continuum of the kind of neighborhood nurturing Maxine had received as a child. In another sense, through observing other black families in need, she was reliving the devastating effects that racism, sexism, and poverty had taken on her own life. Above all, she began to see how she personally could initiate change. The older activist sisters taught her to recognize and value her own feelings and ideas. They also taught her how to find creative solutions to seemingly insurmountable obstacles.

Maxine was eventually promoted to supervisor in charge of coordinating the school's staff of volunteers. About this time, she had her first taste of local politics. Like most energetic, hard-working women who get involved in politics, Maxine entered on the bottom rung, working as a volunteer on local and state campaigns. By 1973, politics was her all-consuming passion.

For her, this was a period of enormous personal growth, as well as enormous personal upheaval. Her marriage ended in divorce in 1972. She was also a student at California State University at Los Angeles, from which she eventually earned a B.A. in sociology. On the political front, Maxine found herself orchestrating David S. Cunningham's successful campaign for a seat on the Los Angeles City Council. Soon after, she was named his chief deputy.

Her experiences at the city council opened her eyes to a new reality: Politics was the most powerful weapon with which to fight endemic racism and poverty. By now, she had fully developed that strong sense of self that characterizes every visionary leader. She no longer needed others to show the way.

"When you start to believe in yourself in a profound way and to understand your own power," she said, "you stop thinking you can't do something because you don't see anyone else doing it. You just think, 'Well, I'll be the first one. I'm going to do it.' You're almost oblivious to the fact that there's no one else there doing it."

Maxine's decision to become a political candidate herself grew directly out of her discovery of inner strength, a kind of personal centering. Her timing was right. New faces were appearing at the nation's leadership table, and they were black women: In 1968, Shirley Chisholm had become the first black congresswoman, followed four years later by Barbara Jordan and Yvonne Brathwaite Burke.

Maxine's opportunity came unexpectedly in 1976, when Leon Ralph, California's incumbent assemblyman representing the Forty-eighth District, a poor community with large black and Hispanic populations, decided not to run. By holding back the announcement of his withdrawal until literally the last hour, Ralph was able to maneuver his hand-picked successor onto the ballot. The ensuing uproar forced the California secretary of state to extend the filing deadline, and provoked Maxine, a wild card, to enter the contest.

Despite the tremendous odds, she scored an impressive primary victory and went on to beat the Republican challenger.

With her election, rumors immediately began to swirl around the state capital. Not knowing what to expect from this "little black woman," the California assemblymen prepared for battle. Maxine didn't disappoint them.

"They referred to everybody as assemblyman in those days," she recalled. "I thought that was odd, that I should be called assemblyman, just like I think it's odd now that someone would call me a congressman. I'm just not. I'm a woman. I thought maybe they hadn't understood that they were supposed to change the wording. So I offered a resolution to change it to 'assemblymember,' so one title would apply to everybody. The place went crazy. They accused me of trying to neuter the men. They carried on for days. It was a big mess. However, eventually the assembly started to call everybody assemblymember, and a lot of things changed as a result of that."

In retrospect, Maxine admitted that part of the overreaction stemmed from fear of the unknown. But assemblymembers were equally foreign to Maxine. She credits one of the nation's most powerful black leaders, Mayor Willie L. Brown Jr., then speaker of the California Assembly, for helping her adjust to the high-powered pressure that accompanies any move onto the political battlefield. Theirs was a positive relationship where a seasoned black male politician showed a young sister the ropes. Reflecting on his teaching role, Mayor Brown said, "I've been a feminist for a very long time, long before it became popular. I've always worked to see that women were assigned key leadership roles. I don't mean heading up social welfare, but committees like budget, finance, and ways and means." Indeed, the leadership experience for Maxine was invaluable, and she had many more lessons to learn.

"Once you start to get into certain kinds of jobs, then you begin to understand the sexism that goes along with the racism. In the legislature I was a threat as a woman, even before I had any power."

Based on what they had heard about her during her years at

the Los Angeles City Council, many of the assemblymembers considered Maxine a maverick at best, and a troublemaker at worst. Those ready to dismiss her point-blank style as pure noise were in for a surprise. Maxine has never made noise just to hear herself talk. From the beginning of her career, substance drove the style. Undaunted by personal criticism, Maxine set about working toward improving the lot of her constituents who were trapped in the system and marginalized by entrenched racial injustice.

From her own experiences of being trapped in low-wage jobs, trying to find affordable child care, and leaving a job because of pregnancy complications, Maxine knew intimately the worries and fears of her female constituents. She helped organize women in her district into action groups, from which they could work for change on their own behalf. Working at the street level, she took the time and poured out the energy. Her efforts expanded to all of Los Angeles. One of her groups became the Black Women's Forum, which she cofounded in 1978 with Ethel Bradley, wife of former Los Angeles Mayor Tom Bradley, and Ruth Washington, publisher of a local black newspaper.

Before long, Maxine earned a reputation as a tough politician prepared to take a stand on hard issues. Her petite size and quick smile belied her strength. She fought relentlessly for jobs and education programs to help the people she represented. Many of the details of this period in Maxine's life can be found in the *Current Biography Yearbook* 1992.

One enduring piece of legislation was Waters's strip-search bill. In 1983, a series of statewide hearings revealed that police officers were strip-searching women and children for minor offenses such as dog license delinquency and traffic violations. Maxine introduced a bill to prohibit strip searching for misdemeanors, and the assembly promptly passed it. But the bill was vetoed by Governor George Deukmejian, who argued that such a law could threaten the security of the state's jail system.

Typically, Maxine did not give up. She appealed for help to the various women's groups that she herself had helped to organize. With their muscle behind her, she pressured Deukmejian into a compromise. A revised bill, prohibiting strip searching unless weapons, drugs, or violence are involved in the alleged crimes, passed quickly through the legislature and was signed into law. This particular example showed her colleagues that she could be both efficient and flexible.

Maxine has boundless energy. She never gives up and she never wears out. The question everyone asks is, How does she do it?

"It's important to have a philosophical ground," she said, "a point of view, something to believe in. People who believe in something and learn to act on it, can win. You can win a lot. People who don't believe in very much, or who are willing to compromise away what they think, never experience the exhilaration of winning in real ways. I act on my beliefs. Oftentimes, I'm able to make things happen because I believe I can."

While Maxine Waters has many inspired moments, her greatest successes seem to come from sustained, passionate effort, like her position early on toward South Africa. While still in the California State Legislature she was among those who worked tirelessly for the passage of a bill barring the state from investing in companies doing business with South Africa. She never missed an opportunity to argue for the bill. Waters introduced the legislation six times over eight years. She never lost heart and she never gave up. Her landmark divestment bill passed in September of 1986.

Other important legislation also passed largely as a result of her efforts. One bill mandated longer prison terms for drug dealers carrying weapons, and another created incentives for those willing to invest in low-income neighborhoods. She also helped to establish the Child Abuse Prevention Training Program, the first of its kind in the United States.

By the mideighties Maxine had become one of the most conspicuous members of the state assembly. Her sensitivity to the unspoken needs of her constituents faultlessly guided her to small hot spots, which always seemed to wind up in the headlines. Whenever she stuck out her public neck, the people of her district (and increasingly many other parts of the state) stood with her, because invariably she was giving articulate expression to their deepest feelings.

On occasions, she seemed to go too far. In 1982, for example, the Democratic-controlled legislature was scrambling to complete a reapportionment bill before Governor Edmund G. Brown Jr. left office. Maxine held up the deliberations by trying to force the removal of the all-white conservative community of Downey from the mostly black Twenty-ninth Congressional District. The Twenty-ninth, which covered much of Maxine's territory, was the obvious district from which she could score a direct congressional hit, if she chose to run—particularly if she could get rid of Downey. The party accused her of jeopardizing its agenda for her own personal gain. Maxine didn't blink: "That's the way the guys do it," she said. But this was a rare moment. For the most part, Maxine's agenda is never to do it "the way the guys do it."

Largely she succeeds, far beyond anyone's imaginings. Even a superficial appraisal of her record shows clearly that her style is merely the by-product of her mission. " 'Confrontational,' they say. 'Activist,' they say. 'In your face,' they say. I describe it as acting on your beliefs."

By the mideighties it was clear to friend and foe alike that her bold initiative and dogged persistence could be neither outclassed nor outmaneuvered. She was the first woman in the state's history to serve as majority whip, the first female member of the Rules Committee, and the first person without a legal degree to sit on the assembly's Judiciary Committee. She also chaired the powerful Ways and Means Committee's Subcommittee on Business Development and Consumer, Veterans, and Employment Issues, where she authored California's first affirmative action bill, which opened up state procurement and contracts to minorities and women. She chaired the Democratic Caucus, and for many years was one of only six legislators serving on the Budget Conference Committee.

Maxine's district returned her to the state assembly for seven consecutive terms. Her uncanny ability to identify and act on molten issues had spread to issues developing far beyond her own district.

By 1989 she was the most powerful woman in California politics, and a political leader of national stature. When Congressman Augustus F. Hawkins announced his retirement from the Twenty-ninth District, after thirty years of service, Maxine swept the Democratic primary, capturing 88 percent of the vote. In November of 1990 she scored a decisive victory in the general election, becoming the second black female from California to be elected to the House of Representatives.

Maxine arrived in Washington with a clear set of goals: ridding her communities of drugs, creating new educational programs, job training, and employment opportunities. These were issues crucial to the future of her people. On the international front, she staked out South Africa for her special attention.

To accomplish her agenda, she knew she would have to work within the system, which for her meant changing the system's rules, rather than adapting herself. "Just because the world has always been defined in one particular way doesn't mean that you have to fit into that model," she said. "It's a lesson that people of color must learn.

"If the usual route to the Capitol is down this hall, down those steps, and out the door, you may have to find a new route. Because every time you go down that route, it's filled already. Everybody's ahead of you. And all those people ahead of you get to the Capitol and get the goodies first. So, you've got to find a new route, make new rules—redefine the ways things are done."

In Congress Maxine continued to behave in the same forthright manner that had served her well all of her life. Her style, she says, was not a matter of choice, but rather a natural extension of her inner persona. "I didn't try to hide it, and I didn't try to redefine myself. As I moved up the ladder, there were a lot of things that I learned to do. But my style was not one of them. I brought this with me."

Her first days in Congress were a repeat of her foray into the statehouse. Assigned to the quietly efficient Veterans Affairs Committee, Waters immediately made waves where no waves had gone before. The committee chair, the highly respected G. V. Montgomery, asked all the panel members to vote against any measures that would require new spending. On her first day, Maxine openly challenged him, breaking an unwritten rule of Congress. In the months that followed, she regularly criticized the committee for what she considered its insensitivity to minorities. In November of 1991, Waters fired off a letter to Montgomery demanding that he "enact a substantial affirmative action program" for the committee staff. As usual, the heat of her rhetoric was based on cold facts: only one black person—herself—sat on the thirty-three-member committee, while more than one-fourth of all the men and women in the service were blacks. The clarity of her argument was irrefutable. Two additional black members were added to the committee's staff.

One of Maxine's special gifts is to see the whole picture, including every small detail. When her committee proposed legislation to protect the jobs of veterans of the 1991 Persian Gulf war, she picked up on a seemingly small item that would have significant impact on veterans, who often do not have enough money or clout to pursue their legal rights. She persuaded the panel to attach an amendment to the bill enabling veterans who sue for job discrimination to seek recompense for their legal expenses.

During her service on the panel she succeeded in literally changing the complexion of that body. Her advocacy for veterans, particularly black veterans, also earned the respect of her colleagues, including Montgomery.

Her sensitivity to the feelings of her people occasionally led her into rough seas. When Los Angeles exploded following the acquittal of four white police officers in the Rodney King case, Waters immediately flew from Washington to California. As she saw it, she had a moral responsibility to give voice to the frustrations of victimized black Americans who identified with Rodney King. She was attacked by many journalists and politicians, charging that she was attempting to justify the violence that followed the acquittal. In the many interviews she gave at the time, Maxine staunchly condemned violence. But she also said that privileged Americans failed to understand that the rebellion grew out of the hopelessness that had pervaded urban

America for decades; the jury's verdict had merely been the catalyst. To many black Americans, Maxine Waters was a hero.

Politically speaking, you have to be an insider to get anything done in Washington. The fascinating question is how a rule breaker like Maxine manages to be such an effective insider, without relinquishing her passion or anger over the lot that has been dealt her constituents.

Contrary to popular perception, Waters considers herself an agreeable person. "I start out dealing with everybody in a reasonable fashion," she said. "I can make a proposal and work with people. Up to a point. Then there is a certain point where I do not suffer insult. I do not allow people to disrespect me or step on me. Only when it gets to that point do I exercise what I need to exercise to change those relationships."

If you examine the course of Maxine Waters's achievements, each victory has been won in a series of well-thought-out steps. First, she recognizes a need and understands how lawmaking can improve a problem. She studies all sides of the issue carefully and looks for solutions, which often turn out to be deceptively simple and startlingly original. Then she lays the groundwork, just as she did when she organized women's action groups in California. Only after this careful preparation does she seize the initiative. Once she springs her proposal, she demonstrates her two most underrated characteristics: flexibility and persistence.

No matter what she says about her "agreeable" nature, her style is still somewhat unsettling to the more genteel representatives of Congress. In five short years, she has managed to scare the pants and the skirts off of more than half her congressional colleagues. But while her colleagues are quick to mention her style, they are quicker to praise her effectiveness. Many say, "I respect her—she fights for what she believes in."

Waters covers all of the bases, all of the time. She is trusted and depended upon within her party. She is a member of the Democratic National Committee and has been a delegate or alternate at every Democratic National Convention since 1972. She served as Jesse Jackson's California campaign chairperson during the 1988 presidential election, and as an adviser to Bill Clinton in his successful bid for the Democratic presidential nomination. She seconded Clinton's nomination at the 1992 Democratic convention.

She shuttles between Washington, D.C., and her home in Los Angeles, where she lives with her second husband, Sidney Williams, a former pro football player and businessman who is now ambassador to the Bahamas. Her children are grown and have children of their own, so in certain important circles Congresswoman Waters is known simply as "Grandma."

Perhaps the most inspirational part of the Maxine Waters story is her firm belief that you can do anything if you first "come to grips with who you are." Mental and emotional health are crucial to superior performance. Maxine called it "getting in touch with and attuned" to oneself.

"You must give yourself permission to say things that are often unacceptable," she told me. "You cannot follow the rules of these political institutions. They were created and perpetuated by people who don't look like you. You can't buy their rules, because they will never allow you to do the job that you must do for the people you're trying to rescue."

Though Maxine Waters is enraged by the conditions in which urban Americans live, she also manages to be optimistic about the future—a combination that is political gold. Today, more than ever, she still uses every ounce of blast she can muster. As the conservative Congress crudely pursues a slash-and-burn policy for social programs, Congresswoman Waters refuses to back off. She argues, repeatedly, that something's wrong with a country that prefers to spend billions of dollars on prisons, rather than fund afterschool and work programs for youth. She refuses to endorse eliminating affirmative action programs, and she adamantly refuses to abandon those who need the most help.

Maxine does not always win, but her reaction to losing is the same as her reaction to winning: She is a dynamo that keeps on turning. No matter how bad things are, she believes change is always possible. In every word and deed Maxine Waters proclaims that African Americans are of great and significant value to this country, and she never wavers in her support of her community.

2

Sisters in Charge

There's no need for false modesty. After hundreds of years of being used and abused, overlooked and forced into the background, black women have finally arrived.

—*Shirley Dennis*
Former director of Women's Bureau, U.S. Department of Labor, and former Secretary for Community Affairs, Commonwealth of Pennsylvania

By what mix of alchemy has American society produced, seemingly out of thin air, influential black women such as Maxine Waters? Severely restricted by the triple historical burden of poverty, skin color, and female gender, how could so many individuals so suddenly rise to the top while, despite the African American community's long and proud history of accomplishment against the odds, many others are losing ground.

The lethal combination of unrelieved poverty, urban isolation, and racial discrimination has perpetuated an environment that 130 years after the Emancipation still makes it almost impossible for many blacks to prosper. Despite some gains, the 1990 census painted a bleak picture: African Americans are still underrepresented in the workforce and disproportionately present in the unemployment lines. Unemployment stood at 8.9 percent among blacks, versus 4.3 among whites. We are underrepresented in the nation's colleges and overly represented in the nation's prisons. Thirty percent of college-aged African Americans are enrolled in higher education, versus 43.2 percent for whites. Only 11.9 percent of all blacks have completed four or more years of college, compared to 22.1 percent of all whites.

We tend to occupy the deteriorating sections of America's inner cities, rather than the sprawling suburbs. According to the 1990 census, the poverty rate for black families is 30.4 percent, and fewer than 14.9 percent earn over $50,000 a year. By contrast, the poverty rate for white families is 8.8 percent, and 34.1 percent earn more than $50,000 a year.

Random acts of violence reflect our alienation. Blacks are 11 percent of the total U.S. population, yet 47.3 percent of the population in state prisons is black.

African Americans suffer disproportionately at both ends of life's spectrum. The mortality rate for black infants is 14.4 percent versus 7.7 percent for white infants. Black males and females who were born in 1970 can expect to live 60.0 years and 68.3 years respectively; their white counterparts can look forward to 68 years and 75.6 years respectively.

When you look at the total statistical picture, black women hold the lowest-paying domestic and service jobs and, earning an average of $11,527 annually, are the poorest of all wage-earning Americans. They are the least likely to be married, and the most likely to have their children living with them in poverty. (Fifty-five percent of all black children live in poverty with their mothers.)

These data make it even harder to explain the sudden, unprecedented appearance of African American women in positions of power.

In America today, power is concentrated in the hands of those who have been able, through appointment, election, effort, or mere fortune, to take command of institutions that control and distribute valuable resources. The powerful operate within a complex matrix of interlocking domains: government, churches, the judiciary, the military, the media, business and financial institutions, and national and grassroots special interest groups. The way power is exercised depends on the individual, the resources at his or her command, and the tactical methods available: the "who," "what," and "how." To move around successfully in this territory requires authority, leadership, influence, negotiation, and persuasion, all of which may be used differently in different settings.

Power is a loaded concept. In its broad domain, power reaches from the minute depths of individual ambition and widens to a global context. We speak of personal power, collective power, and community power and argue over the impact of local, regional, and national power on the world as a whole. We recognize the intertwining nature of political power and economic power, and into the mix we toss social power, legislative power, and religious power. We speak of the power of the spirit, the power of love, and the powers that be. There is white power, black power, and power to the people.

By almost any definition of power, black women in America are not in line to grasp it. Historically, society has used stereotypical images as a way to dismiss sisters. Black women were either sexy, sultry Sapphires, or they were Aunt Jemimas. They were portrayed alternatively as "castrating bitches" out to destroy black men or as the backbone of the race, capable of extraordinary feats of survival under humanity's worst system of oppression, what Dr. Julianne Malveaux describes as the "broad-shouldered black woman."

Those sisters who have been able to transcend the stereotypes and secure some of the most coveted positions of power in this country are America's newest social pioneers. In the past, the crossover of certain extraordinary individuals of color into the mainstream has signaled great moments of change in American society: Jackie Robinson in baseball, Marian Anderson in classical music, and Michael Jackson in popular music. Will the movement of black women into mainstream power signal the infusion of fresh talent, which the nation so desperately needs? Sisters are clearly visible, but their presence is still new enough to raise doubts about its permanency. Many people are still surprised and confused merely to see them in places where they have never been seen before.

One recent winter's day a pretty, young black woman carrying a large briefcase under her arm walked into the central rotunda of the House of Representatives in Washington, D.C. Her hair was neatly bound up in two thick braids, and she wore a flowing brightly patterned skirt and gold canvas tennis shoes. As she entered the elevator reserved for House members, the House guard did a double take: "Get off!" he said, alarmed. "You don't belong in here."

He was dead wrong. Thirty-eight-year-old Cynthia McKinney, newly elected congresswoman from the state of Georgia, had a legitimate right to walk in the corridors of power. Yet that right is a slippery thing. Only two years later she would be faced with the threat of losing her hard-won position by the Supreme Court's decision to dismantle her congressional district, citing that it had been drawn along racial lines and was therefore unconstitutional.

Cynthia McKinney and Maxine Waters are two of the forty-five black female leaders whose personal interviews form the foundation of this book. These powerful women had more than high-paying jobs—they had significant control over society's most valuable resources: education, social programs, jobs, funding, housing, business, and justice. Rather than heading up more traditional black female organizations, they were in positions where they represented a broad base of Americans of both sexes and many ethnic and racial groups—blacks, whites, Latinos, Asians, Native Americans, and others. For the most part that meant they were working in mainstream positions where they had the authority to make bottom-line decisions and implement policies that impacted on the lives of others.

They were easy to find. Few major accomplishments by African Americans go unnoticed by the black media. *Ebony*, *Black Enterprise*, *Essence*, and *Black Issues in Higher Education* publish annual lists of the country's most influential African Americans. A review of these periodicals yielded a list of more than one hundred women who matched the above description. All were contacted; some willingly agreed to participate, others did not. Once the interview process was under way, sisters also identified their peers who held similar positions.

The women whose voices are heard in this book were born and raised in every corner of America, but almost all had roots in the South. For the most part, they were living and working in large metropolitan areas that represent the nation's power hubs: New York, Washington, D.C., Chicago, Philadelphia, Atlanta, and Los Angeles.

Their ages ranged from thirty-three to sixty-eight. Most had assumed their current positions after the benchmark age of forty-five. The older women had been early activists in the Civil Rights and labor movements, founding many of the organizations that continue to support women and people of color in the American mainstream today. These women are still pushing the cause forward, with no suggestion of diminished power.

Most of the women fell into the middle-aged group, which meant that they had entered high school or college on the leading edge of integration, and their career choices were widened because of Civil Rights and affirmative action gains, and by the success of the women's movement.

Thirty-three were employed in the public arena, while twelve were leaders in corporate America.

The tone of the interviews was both serious and lighthearted; the women laughed and they wept. Some graphically described their enemies, and many slipped into a sisterly dialogue to share the joys and sorrows that had shaped their life experiences.

The interviews that form the analytic core of this book assailed certain stereotypes that have limited our understanding of black women. These sisters were dedicated, hardworking, and brilliant. As individuals they were greatly similar and greatly diverse, just as their agendas, at first glance, appeared to be both similar and different.

We would expect them to project a high level of self-confidence, and they did. Beyond that, we would not expect to find any perfectly consistent pattern to their lives. Yet, in the complex layering of the details of their lives, these Phenomenal women shared seven core characteristics that made them unique as a group of powerful women. These characteristics will be fully explored in the stories to come. Overall, Phenomenal women were:

1. Enriched from an early age by the strong support of family, church, school, and community.
2. Intensely focused on clearly identifiable goals.
3. Imbued with humanistic values.
4. Politically sophisticated.
5. Profoundly spiritual.
6. Rooted in their own history and self-accepting as blacks and women.
7. Socially conscious and dedicated to a social agenda that transcends personal gain.

No matter how strong the positive personal and environmental supports that characterized the lives of Phenomenal women, there were negative factors that had a tremendous impact on their lives. Their characteristics were only one side of the story. No matter how carefully their parents tried to prepare them, all had been stunned and humiliated by racism. No sooner did they comprehend the nature of racism than they were confronted with the limitations of gender. Sexual discrimination became more pronounced as the women entered the workforce.

The double impact of race and gender discrimination produced many harrowing experiences. Pamela Johnson, formerly publisher of the *Ithaca Journal,* recalled a single moment that crystallized everything she was up against: "It was the high point of my career. I had been interviewed and accepted for employment by a topflight corporation. My spirits were soaring as I left the luxury hotel room where I had been interviewed. When I entered the elevator, a white man propositioned me. He assumed I was a prostitute. He let me know I was still a black female in America."

The confluence of these two forces—a supremely positive childhood preparation swirling against a devastatingly negative tide of racism and sexism—created a mind-set that for some would eventually develop into a new vision of leadership strong enough to surmount almost every obstacle. In a racist, sexist society, they believed they could and should operate at the highest level.

The going was never easy. As they moved up in their careers, they were often brought on board to solve problems others had abandoned as hopeless. One leader in the seminary community said, "A black woman doesn't get to be mayor of a big city until that city is bankrupt." Or, as another woman said, "If a ship is about to sink, then they call in a black woman to save it."

At the same time, each woman lived with daily reminders of being "the first" or "the only." Challenges came from all over: from white men and women who whispered that affirmative action was responsible for the sister's appointment; from brothers who felt that sisters had taken their positions; from sisters who wondered out loud, "Why you and not me?"

The closer they got to the top, the more isolated they became. Personal problems became magnified. Two-thirds of the women were single or had been divorced, a considerably higher rate than among other power brokers. They learned the hard way that most men steer clear of powerful black women. "For all other groups, power is a social attractor," said college president Dr. Vera King Farris. "But for black women, it is a social detractor."

Dark-skinned or light-skinned, heavyset or reed thin, middle-aged or young, black women are not supposed to flourish in the public arena. If by some quirk of fortune they do gain power, they are presumed to sublimate their sexuality in their good works. But as we consider the true nature of black women, we see that it was frequently their ability to express love and passion that enabled them to achieve all they did. Although this passion embraced the larger community, it certainly did not replace their sexual needs and desires.

The majority of the women were mothers, and some still had children living at home. Motherhood was perceived as the most significant and rewarding of their many roles. Like other women with demanding careers they struggled to balance their domestic and professional roles. While some did hire domestic help to make life easier, none could slip easily into the roll of "Ma'am" and employ a "girl" to do the housework.

To survive multiple stressors the women developed some special ways of coping, and these, too, turned out to be important keys to their success.

Their perseverance in the face of formidable obstacles bespoke a passionate commitment to life that can only be described as spirituality. Indeed, every woman interviewed said she relied on faith and the power of the spirit to see her through.

A state cabinet member said, "Nearly everybody up in the governor's cabinet has to go to doctors, psychiatrists, they have to take pills. I don't take nothing. All I do is read my Bible, Psalm 37, 'Fret not thyself because of evildoers. . . . Trust in the Lord, and do good and the sword that the enemy has for your heart will turn and pierce their own.' I never worry. That faith is what brought our foremothers through, our grandmothers through, our mothers through, that's all they had. The Lord will make a way somehow. Cast your burden upon him and leave it right there. And that's what I do. That's how I get through."

Certain similarities among the women were so striking that it seemed possible that they might exercise power in similar ways. However, at first, no particular model was evident. On closer analysis, however, two distinctly different patterns emerged. The investigation clearly showed that not every black woman who managed to reach the top was motivated by the greater good.

This finding felt wrong at first. Many African Americans who came of age in the sixties, when cries for "power" were linked to equality and social justice, suffer from a generational bias. At that time all black leaders were believed to be on a selfless mission to serve their people, a belief rooted in the romantic notion of the greatness of all African people, and the inherent dignity and kindness of people with black skin: In other words, people who have been victimized themselves would never do the same to others. Time revealed a more realistic picture. In this investigation some sisters clearly put individual gain and personal aggrandizement before the welfare of the African American community.

A portion of one interview went like this:

Q: Are you serving on any boards, community councils, or anything like that?

A: Nope.

Q: Are you a member of any organizations?

A: No.

Q: Do you belong to any black organizations?

A: No. I don't belong to anything.

Q: What kind of expectations does the black community have of you?

A: They expect! They are very disappointed sometimes when I am not part of what they are doing. I'm accused of not being part of the community, of not doing anything for blacks. I think that is very unfair [to accuse me] because I think everybody should do for the blacks what they think should be done. I don't object to the lines they form down there to give them baskets of food or whatever it is. But I would not give them that!

Q: Do you have any mentors or role models?

A: No.

Q: Who are your peers?

A: Nobody. Well, maybe Jesus.

This exchange was typical of a small (less than 15 percent) subset of sisters, whom I labeled "Potentiates." I chose this term because, regardless of their present attitude, no safety zone can protect them from racist and sexist assaults, and they always have the "potential" for change.

Potentiates credited their success solely to their own efforts. They appeared to me to be self-centered and at the same time to have low self-esteem. They also seemed reluctant to accept responsibility for their own mistakes. They seemed to be running hard but without a clear purpose or vision. And they were unable to traverse the divide that transforms individual gain into collective achievement for the African American community.

Potentiates held important jobs in business, government, and organizations. Some occupied frontline office positions where their organizations could use them as window dressing.

Many African Americans believe that corporations and institutions often hire token blacks as control agents to keep other blacks in their place. These agents are invariably Potentiates. Many workers share stories about how hard it is to get support from an organization once the "visible" reins of power have been turned over to a sister or a brother. The community can't scream "racism" because a black person is in charge. It is a surefire dilemma.

A growing number of male and female Potentiates are filling new slots created for black folks. Dr. Thaddeus P. Mathis, political scientist and professor of social work at Temple University's School of Social Administration, refers to this frightening phenomenon as the ability of white folks to "grow their own niggers."

Uncovering Potentiates among the group begged the question of what had made these women different from the others. While reasons were hard to pinpoint, it seemed that the process of trying to fit into the mainstream culture at a relatively young age, particularly in college, isolated them physically and emotionally from the African American community while they were still immature. When they began working in predominantly white organizations, they were susceptible to pressures to adopt that organization's values. Mainstream organizations tend to reflect the larger society's racial and gender biases, and young black women inevitably faced competition from everybody. When you throw personal ambition into this mix, it's easy to imagine their vulnerability.

Potentiates pose a serious problem for the black community. If they are accused of being ineffective or corrupt, they counter with charges of racism and/or sexism. (Clarence Thomas's defense against Anita Hill's charges before the Senate Judiciary Committee is a prime example of a Potentiate in action.) It is nearly impossible for white men and women to challenge them successfully. Only the black community can bring them to account.

This is no easy task. The African American community has made many sacrifices to advance its best and brightest. Acknowledging that one may have slipped off the road into the quicksand of unprincipled leadership is painful. Calling them out is bound to be divisive. There is the added danger that we might inadvertently be joining the white power structure—which is viewed as extremely oppressive—to bring down a black leader. African Americans must expand the family forums—the black church, press, civil rights and professional organizations—where sensitive issues about character and integrity among black leaders can be freely discussed. This is the most effective way to challenge questionable actions.

While the existence of Potentiates must be acknowledged, this book is not about them. Once the small subset of Potentiates was identified and separated from the larger group of women, a vastly enhanced picture of the uniqueness of black female power appeared.

The overwhelming majority of the women (85 percent) could be described, in the words of Maya Angelou's poem, as Phenomenal women. They were self-assured, race-conscious sisters who were serious about the business of social justice and social change. They were self-validating. They accepted themselves as blacks and as women, and drew on a wealth of experience and depth of knowledge that reflected both roles. They were deeply committed to their work and dedicated to a social agenda that transcended personal gain. Although most had reached preeminence without any role models, independently each seemed to be creating a new model of leadership with remarkably similar characteristics. Potentiates might be sisters with power, but Phenomenal women had *Sister Power.*

Sister Power begins in the realm of the spirit and spreads itself into a universal, practical commitment to use power in a different way. Sister Power is a concept suggesting that black women will bring new experiences, new insights, and new visions to positions of power.

Overall, black women hold great promise for principled leadership in this country. In many ways they remain a bellwether for our belief system because they are committed to doing something to change the inequality in the American system.

One powerful political woman found herself challenging the state government she had helped put in office.

"When the governor ran for office I was the only black who supported him because he promised to work for social justice. I turned the vote around for him. When his term was over, he wanted the lieutenant governor to succeed him, but this new man told me, point blank, he was going to abolish the affirmative action council.

"I said, 'I'll tell you one thing, you will never be governor of this state if that's your plan.'

"He said to me, 'Who do you think you are, the queen of Sheba?'

"His people begged me, he sent a man to give me $50,000 and I told him it could be a million dollars, I wouldn't support him. Then they offered me the lieutenant governor slot on the ticket. I turned it down for my people."

These women seem to be in the right jobs, at the right times, when and where they are most needed. It was obvious that sisters have abundant nerve and verve. As Shirley Franklin, formerly chief managing director for the city of Atlanta, said, "We are never scared or afraid. We are not a fearful bunch."

None of the Phenomenal sisters sees herself as a superwoman or superhero. Yet it is obvious from their documented histories that they have a clear vision of the future and can articulate their dreams. When others tire of the struggle, they face each new obstacle with energy and conviction.

One thing is clear: Sisters are on a mission. Wherever they serve, they are trying to bring about fundamental changes that will have a lasting impact on American society.

Each woman who participated in this investigation had a fascinating life journey to tell. Because of the limitation of space, I chose eleven of the forty-five life histories to tell in detail, although the voices of many others are also heard. A few have recently changed jobs; their comments reflect their positions at the time of the interview.

The book is organized around the crucial stages and issues of their lives: how they developed in childhood, their experiences once they left the nurturing black community, their professional rise, challenges to their positions, and their struggle for personal happiness. Finally, we see how they are playing out their new leadership model and what it means for us.

In the following chapters we meet women who insisted on their right to self-identity, women who had to create themselves over and over again, women of vision who even now continue to challenge our sense of what is possible.

3

"The Child That Be Talkin' "

My grandmother and my Aunt Pauline were most responsible for shaping my life. And my sixth grade teacher, Miss Bright. She was the one person who pulled out whatever skills and talent you might have had. She believed in the children she taught. Believed we could learn. She never abandoned you and she never gave up.

—*Diane Watson,*
State senator (Calif.)

Without exception, the earliest memories of the women interviewed for this book—regardless of the particulars of their life circumstances—were about the positive, constant attention they received from their parents, teachers, and church folk. Most said they had been consciously groomed for leadership beginning in early childhood.

This was a crucial finding. Their information contrasted sharply with the appealing perception that children growing up alienated from society, without strong parental and school support, can still become high-level achievers if they try hard enough. These sisters had been smart, lively, inquisitive little girls, and their leadership gifts attracted attention from an early age. Their talents were dramatic enough to stand out in both segregated and predominantly white environments.

Gwendolyn Calvert Baker, formerly executive director of the YWCA and currently president of the United States Committee for UNICEF, was born in Ann Arbor, Michigan, in 1934. "At that time the population of Ann Arbor was only about 6 percent black, so I attended white schools. Whenever there was something going on that I felt I needed to address, I'd just do it. I've never been timid. I started being elected to things in elementary school. I can remember being the leader of my sixth grade class and the president of my eighth or ninth grade graduating class. Even in predominantly white situations I always ran with the top, the people who were leading the pack. In most instances I was the only black in that group. I was seen as a leader and respected not only by my peers but also by the teachers and the administration."

Another sister said she eagerly sought leadership even in kindergarten: "My mother tells me I would always say 'I'm the boss . . . please.' I don't know where I got that from, but it was not something my family would put down. They indulged me. So early on I felt that I should be in charge."

Dr. Jewel Plummer Cobb, formerly president of California State University, Fullerton, recalled, "I was always a leader, I was always *told* I was a leader. I was leading when I was in sixth grade."

Emma Chappell, founder and president of United Bank of Philadelphia, was born in Philadelphia in 1941. She was anointed as a "leader" early in her childhood and liked the title. "I was always the head of something. I was class president and things like that. I was president of Sayre Junior High. I remember that I always liked people. I don't think it was politics, it was just that I liked to run for office. Anyhow, I was usually president of this organization or that organization. Whatever I got into."

As little girls, the women were constantly encouraged to develop an array of talents, particularly their public-speaking skills. Dr. Josephine D. Davis, the recently embattled president of York College, was reared in Waycross, Georgia, a small town, where she was born in 1942. "My grandfather was president of the BPU, and I could say the books of the Bible. I can remember this being four and five years old. I was groomed to speak in church. It really was the foundation of my ability."

Josephine attended segregated schools, where she had excellent teachers who did everything possible to develop the talents of their students. "Starting in elementary school and all along the way, my teachers would put me in a program or a play where I'd have to memorize long passages and speak before the public. They always expected a lot from me in terms of how I did my work, how I dressed, how I spoke, how I prepared my lessons, how thorough I was."

Reverend Willie Barrow was born in 1924 in a small town in rural Texas. She attended a one-room segregated school and was its shining star from the time she was big enough to walk. "I started playing the piano when I was about four. Then we had a lot of plays in school and in church. I was in so many that I began to direct them and write them."

There was always more to this early stardom than mere achievement. Whether they were growing up in the twenties or the sixties, these children knew there was a purpose behind the extra attention and support. One said, "All the black children who had anything on the ball were told that they had to achieve. That the race was counting on them, that they had to *do*."

Addie Wyatt, retired vice president of the Amalgamated Meat Cutters Union, who was on the cutting edge of the organized labor movement in the forties and fifties, remembers how growing up in extreme poverty in Mississippi gave her an acute sense of purpose.

"My mother was an excellent seamstress and my father was a tailor. But in the Depression neither could find employment, even though they tried every day. We barely survived on charity. It was humiliating. We were always taught to be proud, so we'd shine up our little shoes on top and put cardboard in the bottom. I remember the day the welfare worker came around and my mother, who was a very precious woman to me, told me to let the woman see that I needed shoes. I was embarrassed for her to see the holes in my shoes. I was sitting up on the little sack of clothes she had brought and I refused to lift up my feet. She pulled my shoes up and my first reaction was to bash her with my feet, because she had humiliated me.

"I realized that we didn't have a decent place to stay. We used milk crates for chairs, five or six of us sleeping in a bed, sometimes going to school with empty stomachs. My mother would promise that when we got home she would have lunch for us, and she was praying and asking God to open some door. I used to ask my mother, 'Why does it have to be like this?' She told me, 'It doesn't. You will have to make a difference, you'll have to do it.' I didn't know what she really meant then, but I certainly did want to make a difference. I didn't like what we had to go through and I wanted to make a change."

Thirty years later, Roberta Palm Bradley, an executive at Pacific Gas & Electric Company, was growing up in a small town in Maryland where her family had lived "for centuries."

"We had always lived in that town, but there were hardly any other African Americans living there. For my first three or four years of schooling I was bused to the town ten miles away to go to a segregated elementary school, even after 1954. My parents were always planning and positioning me as a child for the future. Growing up in the sixties, my core values were developed around breaking the rules and looking to the future."

Halfway across the country, in Indianapolis, another little girl was also growing up with the same forward-looking awareness. Pamela Carter, future attorney general for the state of Indiana, said that as a small child she was fully aware of her incipient sense of self and her future responsibilities. "From the time I was very young, I knew I would make a public impact. I didn't know how and I didn't consciously aspire to it. But it was a given. It's hard to describe, but

I could see it in my mind's eye. It was always sort of a giving back. We were always taught to give back."

The themes of early preparation were deep, broad, and consistent among the women. Paula Banks, who today is president of the Sears Foundation, a multimillion-dollar philanthropic arm of Sears Roebuck, Inc., has vivid memories about the ways in which her parents deliberately prepared her for leadership, despite personal tragedy.

"I was a sick child. I had a bone condition and was in and out of hospitals for years. I didn't go to school at all for a couple of years. My parents continued to say, 'You can become whatever you want to become.'

"I walked on crutches. I remember the day the doctor said that I could continue to use crutches, or I could go into a wheelchair. At least with the crutches I was on my feet and mobile; but he said if I used the wheelchair I might eventually walk straight and be healthier. 'What do you want?' he asked. I was only eight years old, but my parents allowed me to make the decision. There was something about the way they said, 'We're going to help you make decisions about your life so that you're the best that you can be.' That's all I ever remember them saying. They always supported taking risks and chances. I told them I wanted to go into the wheelchair. I stayed in it for three years."

Mothers, grandmothers, aunts, and other informally adopted female kin were the architects of the future. The early life experience of Mary Hatwood Futrell, who grew up to become president of the 1,806,000-member National Education Association, gave a vivid picture of her mother's undying dedication to the success of her daughters.

Mary was born on the eve of World War II in the little town of Alta Vista, Virginia. Her mother, Josephine, was a domestic worker, and her father was a construction worker. Mary remembers her early childhood as financially "secure" until her father fell suddenly ill. "My father had to go to Lynchburg for treatment because Alta Vista didn't have adequate hospitals. We didn't have insurance. My mother was going back and forth to Lynchburg and was losing time from work. She couldn't keep up the payments on our house, and she ended up selling off the furniture just to keep us alive. We had no one to help us. We ended up losing everything."

Mary's father was in and out of the hospital for a year. He died in 1945, when Mary was four years old. The loss was a devastating blow to the family.

"My mother refused to go on welfare. She refused to take any kind of help. She earned about fifteen dollars a week on her full-time job as a domestic worker. She supplemented that by working as a short-order cook, and working as a day cleaner, going from house to house to earn enough to support us. She held all three jobs all the time and worked seven days a week, eighteen hours a day. It took her eight years to pay my father's medical bills. But she was determined to do it.

"Years passed before we could spend a Christmas together because my mother always worked on holidays. We rarely went to church together because she worked on Sundays. But she made sure my sister and I went."

These were hard years, but Mary and her older sister, Ann, learned valuable lessons. "We learned to take care of ourselves. We knew we had to get up and go to school in the mornings, come home and have certain chores completed. I remember vividly my mother leaving lists of things for us to do and they had to be done by the time she arrived back."

When Josephine was forced to spend long days away from home, the community moved in to fill the void. "Our neighbors knew how difficult my mother's schedule was, so they kept an eye on us. When you're growing up you resent that. You resent the neighbors telling Mama that you didn't do the chores you were supposed to, that you went outside and played, that you had friends come over to the house. I can remember getting upset with neighbors who would tattle on us. We resented it because maybe we didn't always do what we were supposed to do. But now I appreciate what they did.

"Those women looked out for us. They made sure that you did your chores, did your homework, and they looked out for whoever was coming into the house. 'Mary and Ann, you know you're not supposed to have so and so in the house! We know what's going on!' And they would pop up any old time.

"But they were also the ones—if we needed any food, if we needed something done, maybe somebody got sick or something like that—they were the ones who were asking, 'Did you have dinner? Have you had lunch?' They were the ones who provided the extra base of support.

"The church folk also participated. I remember they used to take trips to Coney Island, New York, and places like that, and they would make sure there was enough money for us to go, too. Somebody was always there to look after us."

Throughout her childhood, Mary observed her mother's tremendous strength and tenacity in everyday living, and realized how much fortitude a black woman needed merely to survive in America. Even as Josephine struggled to take care of her daughters, she reached out and took in two more little girls who had been orphaned. "My mother was good friends with their mother, and when their mother passed away my mother raised them." By her mother's example, Mary learned to appreciate the African American tradition that extends itself to all children in need.

Josephine herself had been orphaned as a young child, and by the age of fourteen was already supporting herself working as a domestic. She did not want her girls to be trapped in a similar cycle of poverty. The best guarantee she could provide was making sure they got a good education. "My mother put a lot of emphasis on education because she wanted to make sure we did not end up having unskilled jobs and having to work as hard as she did. She wanted us to have a better life, and education was the answer.

"I attended Pane Elementary School, which was a segregated

school in Lynchburg. All the way through elementary and secondary school we had dedicated, well-educated teachers who were determined that we would succeed. They did not accept being a minority, or poor, or female as an excuse not to learn. We were required to meet their very high expectations. They were demanding and watchful."

Despite Josephine's exhausting work schedule, she always found time to pay attention to her daughters' schooling. "My mother didn't have a car, but she would come to school, sometimes changing buses two or three times, just to see how we were doing. She didn't go on just back-to-school night or PTA night. It was any old time she would show up.

"My mother made sure the homework was done every night. She would say, 'I don't care how tired I am when I come in, the homework has to be on the table!' She knew when the report cards were due. She found time to come to school if we were in activities. We were always aware that she cared about the education we received and that she was working closely with our teachers. She did what she was supposed to do, and we did what we were supposed to do." Undoubtedly all of these emotional experiences influenced Mary's future career choices.

At that time, simply finishing high school was considered an important achievement. When she finished high school Mary had no plans to go to college, but unbeknownst to her, her teachers were making plans for her. "The teachers in my school, even those who didn't teach me directly, went out into the community, to the churches, businesses, civic organizations and various groups giving grants and scholarships and said, 'We have a young lady we would like to send to college and she doesn't have the finances. We would like you to help us send her.' I didn't know that until the night I graduated."

Mary Hatwood Futrell went on to graduate from Virginia State University, and did her graduate work at George Washington University, University of Maryland, University of Virginia, and Virginia Polytechnic Institute and State University.

Mary's childhood experiences taught her lessons about overcoming adversity that she carries to every child growing up in America today: "You can't allow the negatives to overwhelm you. If you let yourself become focused on those incidents you fail to see the larger picture, and you don't make the difference."

With some personal variations, the larger themes of Mary Hatwood Futrell's story were repeated in the lives of all the black women interviewed. As they spoke of their parents, teachers, and churches, they spoke with one voice.

Reverend Willie Barrow, the beautiful and dynamic chairman and CEO of Operation PUSH (People United to Serve Humanity), grew up in a large extended family on a farm in Texas in the twenties and thirties. Her parents grew cotton, corn, and garden vegetables, and raised hogs and chickens. "We were poor, but I never knew hunger. We used to go and pick cotton for other people to supplement our income. There were seven children. Both of my grandmothers and my great-grandmother lived with us. My father's youngest brother lived with us. We went to work as a family, we cleaned as a family, and we went to church together.

"My parents were extremely strict, and I couldn't do what a lot of other young people were doing. I couldn't smoke. I couldn't go to the movies. I couldn't even dance, they were so strict. I didn't go out with a boy until I was over seventeen years old. We always had to go as a group.

"I thought the sun rose and set on my schoolteacher. From the time I started first grade on up, until I went to high school, I wanted to grow up to be Miss Kinnard. On birthdays my mother had to bake the best kind of cake for me to take to my teacher. She was my God.

"The other teacher I could never forget was Willella Sparks. And my Sunday school teacher. I thought those women—I liked the way they dressed. I liked the way they talked. I liked the way they stood. I wanted to be just like them.

"I used to line up dolls and teach classes. When we didn't have dolls I would take sticks of wood and dress them up with bandannas and put little caps and stuff on them and line up my class and teach like Miss Kinnard."

Unita Blackwell, the first black mayor in the state of Mississippi, was born into a family of sharecroppers in Lula, Mississippi, in 1933, in the depths of the Depression. Nobody could have been poorer or had less opportunity. "My father was a man who believed in taking care of himself and his family. When the boss tried to put me into the fields at a very young age, my father stood up. He had to move out of the state because he got into it with the boss man.

"My mother had the determination to make sure that we got some kind of what she called education so you could be 'somebody.' Now, being somebody, in her mind, was just being able to stand up and possibly, maybe one day, just try to take care of yourself, where you could read, write, and count."

Blackwell's aunt and grandmother were also strong, capable women. In the midst of their daily struggle to survive, the older women in Unita's family encouraged her to learn how to play the piano and develop an appreciation for the arts.

"My teachers were so important. I can remember Miss Franklin saying to me, 'You can do it.' This was when I had to get up and make a speech. The children would come together and each class would participate by having somebody get up and talk or do something. We would now call it 'learning to communicate.' Miss Franklin did a fantastic job of pushing me out there in the world. I don't know what she did about my English. She had good English, but I don't have it. She had me get up and say a speech or a poem every Friday. I'd put my hands together and say this poem, and smile. Children were sniggling and laughing at you. We called it sniggling.

"In my family you had to learn how to get along with people, and interact with folks, and also stand your ground. My family was a thinking family who knew that just because you were white, you didn't have to be right. My mother and grandmother believed that God made us all and we should try to find a way to stand up. But they didn't call it that. They were people with guts, that's what they used to call it. They would just speak up."

She recalled a family folktale about her grandmother. "My grandmother used to work for the white man. She was a great cook, but she wanted to learn to read. When the woman said, 'Mammy, what are you putting in the food?' Mammy said she didn't know, she just threw in a little of this and a little of that. She told the white woman that she needed some cookbooks so she could get better recipes. The woman started to get her books, and pretty soon Mammy—she was reading! I came up with that kind of thinking family."

Josephine D. Davis believed that her family was prosperous and well educated. The women particularly stood out as remarkable achievers in an era when women of every color and class had few opportunities for education and careers. "I come from a heritage of proud, strong women. These are the images of my childhood. One of my aunts was a principal. She had two sons who graduated from college, one of whom became a surgeon. We had female role models in my family—educators, administrators, a nurse on my mother's side. I had a great-aunt who traveled to China and Japan. My paternal grandmother was an evangelist, always on the road in the countryside. She was commuting and her husband was raising the children. This was in the thirties and forties."

Gwendolyn Calvert Baker, growing up in the industrial area of Ann Arbor, Michigan, in the thirties and forties, also admired and modeled herself after her grandmother.

"She was a very gracious woman. She was the kind of woman who never sat down without a tablecloth, a cloth napkin, and sterling silver napkin rings. She had polished hardwood floors, those kinds of things. She had learned about these things by working as a domestic in very wealthy homes. She often took me to work with her. I would sit in the kitchen and shine fruit or whatever, sometimes I played with the children in the family. I learned to eat frog legs at an early age because I was exposed to good food and the niceties of life by going to work with her. She would buy me white gloves and dress me and treat me like the rich white people treated their children.

"So I grew up viewing my grandmother as a very ladylike, genteel type of person, and I wanted to be like her. She was a beautiful woman. She was the one I patterned after."

While mothers and grandmothers were powerful role models for virtually all of the women, many also received strong support from their fathers and grandfathers. Pamela Carter, future attorney general for the state of Indiana, was born in South Haven, Michigan, in 1946, and grew up in Indianapolis. Both of her parents were community activists. "My father held a number of jobs, but what I remember most is that he was a businessman, he owned a janitorial service. He was a coach, and because of him I was involved in a lot of athletics."

Pamela was also greatly influenced by her paternal grandfather. "He was an ordained minister, African Methodist Episcopal, but he actually had studied law. He would quote the law to me when I was a child, because he had memorized all of it. He had come up on his own, which was a treacherous experience, and became quite a force in his community. Although he had studied law he was not allowed to practice in Indiana because of his skin color."

Several women had parents who were teachers, ministers, or even physicians. The grandparents of Floretta McKenzie, superintendent of the Washington, D.C., school system, were physicians at the turn of the century.

In the black community this group was viewed as the upper class, even though its members often didn't have the economic rewards that go along with their social status. When these women talked about their family status, they used the terms "middle class" and "working class." Even those who didn't have that kind of social standing, and even those who grew up poor, also described their families as "kinda middle class."

While the community is far from monolithic, historically there have been only two groups—those who worked and those who didn't. In the first half of the twentieth century, the majority of blacks were employed, as they are today. Having any kind of job was likely to place you in the middle class. If you could feed your family, shelter them from harm, and reduce the debilitating effects of economic exploitation, you were not poor. Your wealth was derived from positive life experiences.

Josephine D. Davis, who considered her family well off, shed light on the difference between the white community's and black community's perception of class:

"We were actually quite poor, although I didn't know it. Being economically poor is different from being poor in spirit. I thought we were middle-class people. Both of my parents were high school graduates. My father was a smart man. Everybody always came to him for whatever. He did their income taxes, he repaired things, he did electrical work. He was a brilliant man. He would help me with my homework, motivate me.

"But we lived in a wood house on a dirt street, we had to walk everywhere we had to go. I worked in the tobacco fields. I worked in the cotton fields. My mother worked as a maid.

"That movie, *Imitation of Life*, I could identify with everything. My mother was like that maid, she would cook, clean. Then she worked in a hotel, cooking. Then she worked in a factory. We always had food on the table, and I don't remember wanting for anything.

"I always thought we were doing well. Until I went to Spelman College. It was my senior year and I will never forget it. I took a sociology class, and I can remember the day, I get chills thinking about it, when the professor described people whose parents were laborers, whose income was such and such, in the rural South, and said they were 'underprivileged.'

"That had major psychological impact. It troubled me tremendously. Because in my mind we were rich. As I look at the current generation of black youth now, I think the language of sociology has had a tremendously negative impact on them. They grow up thinking of themselves as disadvantaged. Their minds, their spirits, are impoverished. My upbringing was no different from theirs, but mine was a bountiful spirit and we had plenty."

Most of the women projected this sense of a contributing working family, whatever positions or jobs their parents or grandparents held. The people they viewed as "lower class" were those who couldn't hold even the most menial jobs. However, in the black community the line between middle and lower class could be very thin indeed.

Emma Chappell, the future president of United Bank of Philadelphia, described how fragile the boundaries were. Her parents, George and Emma Lewis Bayton, worked as chefs for Horn and Hardart in Philadelphia, the famed automat chain that took the country by storm in the forties. Her parents owned their home at Fifty-ninth and Race Streets in west Philadelphia. This was an early period of home ownership for black folks, which followed World War II. Emma said, "We were definitely considered middle class because of home ownership and two jobs, especially in those years."

Emma's mother developed a serious heart condition and died when Emma was fourteen. "We were really just surviving by that time, because we had been paying a lot of medical bills. My mother's insurance had run out, and when she died, my father wasn't sure how he was going to pay all the bills. I wasn't the oldest child, but I was the oldest daughter, so I assumed my mother's role.

"My father worked all the time. I would go to school, come home and work, and try to keep the family together. At that time the child welfare workers were talking about taking us away from my father because they weren't accustomed to men playing the mother and father roles. They conducted some sort of investigation around the neighborhood. The neighbors told them what a good family life we had and so there was no problem. We all stayed together."

Fortunately, Emma received continual support from neighbors, schoolteachers, and the church. She was smart, energetic, and enterprising. No matter how oppressive the conditions became, Emma always found a way to make the best out of it. She excelled in school, and there was little doubt in anyone's mind that she would emerge as a productive citizen.

The families of all of the women believed that education was the road to success. Many were also politically committed and dedicated to public service. Cynthia McKinney was born in 1956 in Lithonia, Georgia. Her mother, a nurse, and father, a Georgia state legislator, instilled a commitment to education, responsibility, and public service. Cynthia's family was politically active at a time when standing up for one's rights and freedom could be deadly. She learned through observation that the basic struggle for human rights was an ongoing part of the black experience, and that it was important to do your part. From childhood, Cynthia's methods of leadership were always unorthodox. In the eighth grade she tried to overthrow the faculty and install student leadership in its place. The school threatened to expel her, but she was saved by her mother, who convinced the nuns to give the instigator another chance.

Marcia Gillespie, future editor in chief of both *Essence* and *Ms.* magazines, said her family also thrived on political action. Marcia was born in 1944 in Baldwin, Long Island, New York, into what she describes as a black southern community within a white suburban community, or what is sometimes referred to as "upsouth." In this insular enclave, Marcia said, almost everybody seemed to have come from the same twelve towns in North Carolina.

Both of her parents were voting rights activists and both assumed leadership roles in civic and social organizations. "My family helped to push one of the first public education integration systems in the state of New York." The elementary school that would later receive young Miss Gillespie had been integrated as a result of a lawsuit brought by her family.

By the time Marcia arrived, the school was drawing from a broader base of students. Here, her own leadership potential began to show itself. "I was class president in elementary school," she said. "You could see it coming."

Marcia described her father as having a fourth grade education, and an unquenchable thirst for knowledge. Her mother, Ethyl, was a Long Island native, with firm ties to black northern traditions. "My mom did housecleaning and then had a catering business on the side. She was also president of the Board of Better Education in this very upper-middle-class, predominantly white community." In spite of her limited education, Ethel established a formidable presence in the community. "You're not to mess with Ethel Gillespie's children, you understand what I mean? It was serious. People who think they have to wait until they have an education or they have to wait to have money to do this or that—uh, uh, no way. Not my Mom."

All through school, Marcia practiced her public speaking and "get-along skills" to maintain her leadership. At South Side High School in Rockville Center she was vice-president of the student government. She received constant reinforcement from her family, friends, and members of the community.

"I grew up in a very supportive circle. My grandmother lived at the other end of the block. That is where I went after school, to Nanna's. She was just all love. She always gave me the sense that 'I was the smartest and the bestest.' Do you know what I mean?

"I grew up in a family that encouraged their children to think, to have opinions, to talk about them, sit around the dinner table and have debates. Even when I was eight years old, my father would say, 'What do *you* think, baby?' I was supposed to be thinking about *something*. I always knew these were people who would have walked through a fire for me."

Marcia remembers she was fully aware of her strengths, yet she was always cognizant of the nature of the real world. She carefully watched her mother and her Nanna and modeled herself after them. "I grew up knowing that if you want change, you did things. That's real important."

If family and school were their chief supports, there was also a third: the church. It is impossible to overestimate the huge debt all of the women said they owed to their churches. Every woman I spoke with had been active in a church as a child, and several had parents or grandparents who were ministers. Most belonged to Protestant denominations, but a few were brought up as Catholics and at least one was Jewish.

Marcia Gillespie lived right next door to her Baptist church, which her grandmother had helped to found. "I grew up singing praise songs. I was one of those kids . . . I remember asking my Sunday school teacher, 'Well, if God split Adam and Eve, where did we come from? After she washed my mouth out with soap, I remember going home saying, 'I'm not going back.' But my parents said, 'You have to.' Church was always part of my life. Not optional."

For many women church was more than a religious observance; it was a forum for political and social activism. Shirley Franklin's church was one of the oldest African American Episcopal churches in the country. "On Sundays we always heard a lot of conversation about how individuals could make a difference in the world, both through their financial contributions, but more importantly through their political persuasion and point of view. The church I belonged to was founded by a very great black religious leader, Absalom Jones. I remember going through confirmation in that church and being very pleased to be associated with such a distinguished African American, even though obviously I never met him."

Emma Chappell's church was Zion Baptist, the center of organized Civil Rights and protest activities in Philadelphia. Her grandparents were one of the original families that helped to organize the church at Broad and Venango Streets. When Emma was a young child, the church hired a fiery young pastor named Leon Sullivan. In the early sixties, he launched the Fisher's boycott, protesting discrimination at the famous eatery on North Broad Street. He founded Opportunities Industrialization Centers of America (OIC), a Booker T. Washington–style, self-help training program. In 1971, he authored the Sullivan Principles, a human rights declaration that provided guidelines for American corporations doing business with South Africa. And in the heart of drug-ravaged North Philadelphia, Sullivan built the Progress Plaza Shopping Center and the Zion Home for Retired Citizens. Reverend Sullivan's activism established Zion Baptist Church as a model of social resistance. This was Emma Chappell's "local church," and it still is. Sullivan's example instilled in her an eagerness to join the battle for human dignity, and proved that individuals working together for a common cause could eradicate massive injustice. She has never changed her mind.

The crucial themes of childhood were consistent among all these powerful black women. Regardless of their economic situation, regardless of the times in which they were born, and regardless of whether they went to poor, segregated schools or more privileged, predominantly white schools—all of the little girls were nurtured and profoundly loved by their parents, particularly their mothers and grandmothers, and admired by their teachers. Their gifts had been recognized and appreciated.

The way these sisters described their early lives differs significantly from the public's perception that all African American families consist of maladjusted, drug-ravaged ghetto dwellers. None of these women claimed to be survivors of dysfunctional, loveless families and communities. Their experiences, as we have seen, contradict the popular notion that young people growing up in severely impoverished and destructive circumstances can become high-level achievers if they just try hard enough. Their stories demonstrate that they need much more than that to succeed.

These sisters had been groomed from childhood to excel. Some were poor, and a few were impoverished, but many came from stable, two-parent families and had childhoods that were emotionally, if not always financially, secure.

Without exception, family unity was central to their upbringing. A few had lost one parent through premature death or abandonment, but the surviving parent and extended family formed a secure safety net. Regardless of financial background or parental status, they lived in communities where other adults cared and shared responsibility for the next generation.

This investigation showed conclusively that it is no happy accident that these sisters landed in positions of power. From their youngest days, all had been told by *someone* that they were special. Parents, teachers, religious leaders, and neighbors recognized their talents and encouraged them to achieve. They had been encouraged to speak out in public practically from the time they learned to talk. They were often described as the "child that be talkin' " and were given opportunities to hone their public-speaking skills in school, church, and community activities. Each had been trained and educated to do her best. Qualities that foster independence, initiative, responsibility, and the ability to follow through had been defined for them and encouraged. All of this was fully entwined with an active church life, which would play an unusual role in the difficult passages to come.

This discovery doesn't mean that young black girls growing up without all of these benefits are destined to fail. On the contrary, the findings point out that the black community can provide a nurturing foundation for emotional and spiritual growth, which leads to a strong sense of identity and a high level of self-esteem. For Phenomenal women these were the critical keys to success.

4

I Can Tell You the Exact Moment

I was mocked and ridiculed at school when I said I wanted to grow up to be president of the United States, just like Abraham Lincoln. I ran home crying to my mother. She very gently told me that I shouldn't expect to be president because I was black and because I was a girl. But her hidden message was, if you want to make something of yourself, you will have to try harder and do better.

—*Wynona Lipman*
State senator (N.J.)

Even the most nurturing family and strongest community support cannot protect a black female child from the realities of racism and sexism in America. The dual onslaught against their self-esteem and future achievement was unescapable. This general theme reverberated in the stories of all the women interviewed: As young girls, they felt the secure foundation of the African American family and community beneath them. But as soon as they set foot into the wider world, even if it was only in the next block, they discovered that their country discriminated against them.

African American parents have always had the painful task of preparing their children for the tough transition. Awareness of racism usually came first, often when they were still young children.

Paula Banks, the child bound to a wheelchair, recalls when she first realized she was "different" from many other little girls. "I can tell you the exact moment. My mother was giving me a bath. I was six years old and she was kneeling by the tub as she always did, in one of those big tubs, and I was playing. I had my dolls laid out around the tub and I was telling my mother about a little girl I had seen on television. 'I'm just like her,' I said.

"My mother said, 'No, you are not!'

"She explained to me that I was black and I was not white. I became hysterical. All my dolls were white and I was clearly being told that I was black. I just didn't believe it. At that age, looking at your skin wasn't as much the issue as, 'I look like that little girl, don't I?' Thinking about it now I think, well, 'You had to be a pretty dumb kid!' "

Dr. Deborah Prothrow-Stith, who at the age of thirty-three became the youngest ever commissioner of public health for the Commonwealth of Massachusetts, vividly recalled her struggle to understand "color" in the fifties: "I remember when I was about five I asked my mother to show me some colored people. We were on our way shopping, the whole family—my mother, father, sister. They parked the car and talked to me seriously for a long time. They told me that we were colored, and the people we knew were colored. I said, 'No, that's not what I'm talking about.'

"Finally, weeks later, I was looking at a magazine and saw a picture of the Jolly Green Giant. I called my mother and said, 'This is it! Colored people!'

"Obviously, they got a kick out of that. But when I think about that, it reminds me of how aware they were about issues of race. 'This is the way the world is,' they said. 'This is how people are treating people. This is what we're doing to try and change it.' "

Congresswoman Corrine Brown (D-Fla.) was born in 1946 in Jacksonville, Florida: "We used to go riding in the car on Sundays. This root beer place that served hamburgers and stuff was on Main Street. My brother and I ran up to the counter and wanted to order root beer, and this woman said, 'We don't serve niggers.'

"I was very young. But I'll never forget it, because we said, 'We're not ordering any.' "

Mary Hatwood Futrell's mother fortified her for the future by teaching her never to use racist language. "In Lynchburg in the forties and fifties the neighborhoods were actually more desegregated than people believe. Although no whites actually lived on our street, they did live on the street that ran perpendicular to it. We played with those little white kids. I remember one time a black guy was walking through the neighborhood. He asked us, 'What are you niggers doing playing with those honkeys?' I remember asking my mother what was a honkey? I already knew what a nigger was. My mother asked where did I hear that, why was I asking that question? When I told her, she said, 'I don't want you using those words.' "

Childhood innocence in simply asking color questions was soon replaced by harsher encounters. Unita Blackwell clearly remembers her first confrontation with a racist. She was eight years old, and he was even younger.

"I was in what they used to call 'white town,' across the tracks from where my aunt lived. That's where the post office was, all the businesses, and things were there. Black people stayed on the other side of the tracks, but we had to go to white town to do our shopping. I went down to do that. This little white boy came up to me and went to screaming, 'Nigger, nigger, nigger, nigger!' And you know how you feel . . . strange. He had such a hateful way of looking at me, because my skin is very dark . . . an old black thing. I was aware before, you know, from listening to mamma talk. But that day this whole phenomenon hit me."

Mary Hatwood Futrell discovered that there was more to racism than bad words when she tried to earn money to help her family by working as a domestic. She was twelve years old. "Sometimes I worked alone, sometimes with my sisters. We worked for private families, and sometimes they would travel from Lynchburg to North Carolina, which is about a six-hour ride. The people with whom we were traveling would have to go inside a restaurant to get food and bring it out to us. If we wanted to go to the bathroom, we had to go out in the bushes."

Fran Farmer, former president, Operation Crossroads Africa, recalled, "We traveled a lot by car, carrying a little potty because if there were black bathrooms they were so funky. When we were driving through corners of Mississippi and Arkansas, I recall my parents locking up the car and telling us to get down, hoping that nobody would bother us. And cops pulling my father over and saying, 'Nigger, what are you doing in this part of the world?' "

Their racist experiences were not limited to the segregated towns of the Deep South. Sisters from various parts of the country spoke of their anguish when they were denied admission to the brand-new YWCA swimming pool, described as niggers and jungle bunnies, and rejected from whites-only Girl Scout troops. Truly, it was a nationwide phenomenon, present in every region and every decade of American history. Their memories of early racist encounters were so vivid that the chorus of voices cannot be hushed:

Roberta Palm Bradley of Pacific Gas & Electric: "I'll tell you something that lives with me until this day. I was probably eight, growing up in an all-white town in Maryland in the fifties. All my friends were white. It was a small town that didn't even have a movie theater. As long as my brother and I were in town, we were treated just like any other child. This was before desegregation. We drank at the water fountains just like all the other children. But when you went ten miles away, there were more black people and there was segregation.

"The movie theater was in Frederick, eight miles away. The aunt of one of my girlfriends piled us into the car and we went to the movie theater. I'm average height now, but when I was eight, I was tall for my age. When we got to the movie theater, the ticket taker asked, 'Are you the baby-sitter?'

"I said, 'No. They're my friends.'

"He said, 'Well, you'll have to sit upstairs in the colored section.'

"Throughout the whole movie, I had to sit upstairs in the Jim Crow section while my friends sat downstairs. It was horrible. It was the defining moment of my growing up."

Dorothy Brunson, CEO of Brunson Communications Inc., and the only black woman in America to own three profitable radio stations in three major American markets: "I can remember a time when you couldn't try on the clothing in a famous department store in New York City, and I can remember very clearly my aunt picketing in front of the store. Thereafter, we were able to try on the shoes."

Some powerful racist messages were quite subtle. Josephine D. Davis remembered eagerly taking her new schoolbook into her hands on her first day in the fourth grade. When she opened it to record her name inside, she saw this stamp: "Discarded from the public schools of the state of Virginia."

She realized immediately something was not right. "Why couldn't I get new books? I lived in Georgia. Why were my books discarded from the state of Virginia?" It was typical at that time for black schools to receive hand-me-downs from white schools. These books were ragged from use before they ever came into the waiting hands of a black child. Even though her book had been discarded by others, Josephine opened it, studied it, and mastered it.

For her, this was the "critical moment" that many of the women mentioned, the moment when they had sudden awareness that the world was inexplicably unfair. Josephine's experience made such an indelible impression on her that it may have provided the underlying motivation that guided her toward a superlative career in education.

Pamela Carter was eight years old when she integrated a Catholic Youth Organization (CYO) camp. "I was the only black there, and I was called a number of names, some of which I didn't realize I was being called because I had never heard those terms before.

"The camp held a meeting, and I was smart enough to know that they had everyone else in the room there except me. Now, my parents are very proud African Americans and I got that pride. I got a little bit of 'oomph,' so I knew that there was something going on. That camp was my first experience with a totally different culture. I wasn't necessarily impressed with it, or not impressed. It was just different. I understood there was an underlying hostility, but I endured. I came out as Camper of the Week. I think they thought I withstood more than I did."

Every child, black or white, growing up in the forties and fifties had their racial perceptions shaped by the movies. Black children who saw Tarzan movies, for example, in which Africa was depicted as a wild, dark, savage continent with a white man as its only saving grace, found it hard to take pride in their heritage. Like all children of that era, Josephine Davis was an avid filmgoer. "Tarzan was the thing you saw, and there were witch doctors with feathers on their caps. I was always embarrassed about these Africans."

However, these young black girls never internalized the racist perceptions that surrounded them. Invariably, they had already developed such a strong sense of self-worth that by the time they became aware of the racist beliefs of the larger society they were able to deflect the most damaging effects.

Shirley Dennis, who was born in 1938 and grew up to become director of the Women's Bureau of the U.S. Department of Labor, remembered: "I lived in the Bronx, where there were only three or four black kids in the entire school. This was during the late forties, right after World War II, before the Civil Rights movement. Certainly there was no 'black is beautiful' movement to counter the presumption that white supremacy was the way it was.

"I was the only black child in my class, and I had to figure out where did I fit. While I wasn't bombarded with the race issue every day, when it was time to have class plays and all of the other things that identified you as a human being, the question was, 'What to do with Shirley?'

"When we did our history lessons, blacks were never mentioned, except as slaves. But I would constantly get some of the best grades in class. So I reasoned that there was something wrong with the concept of white supremacy. Because if white supremacy was a fact, then why was I smarter than 95 percent of these white kids in my class? I decided way back then that white supremacy was not a reality. I recognized that I was a very smart child who could outdo most whites who I went to school with, one-on-one."

Experiences such as these followed the young girls throughout childhood, right up until they stood on the verge of womanhood. C. Delores Tucker, who grew up to become secretary of state of Pennsylvania and chair of the Democratic National Committee Black Caucus, recalled: "My father took me to the Bahamas for my nineteenth birthday, and we went over on the boat from Miami. That evening they told us to go down onto the lower deck of the boat, where all the blacks were. I said, 'Daddy, why do we have to go down there?'

"He said, 'That's where we have to go.'

"I said, 'Why? Why can't we go above?'

"He told me because we were what we were. I said, 'I'm not going down there!'

"And I didn't go. I laid up there outside all night and got pneumonia, and that developed into pleurisy. All of those things made me very, very bitter."

Racism was indeed a bitter pill, and they refused to swallow it. But it was not just simply a question of race. There was also a subcategory called "color," and one's location on the color spectrum elicited different kinds of responses, even within the black community.

Cynthia McKinney, at age thirty-eight the youngest black woman in Congress, encountered "color" in elementary school: "My first experience in realizing that race was a major problem came not from the white community, but from the black community, which discriminated against people who had dark skins. I remember feeling inferior to my classmates whose skin was light. Now, why should I feel inferior when I'm a better student, when I'm worthy of the same consideration? We had the same incomes. We all went to private Catholic school. The teachers, who were white nuns, looked at us all the same. Whether we were light skinned or dark skinned, we were still black as far as they were concerned. That was my first experience with discrimination. It didn't come from white folks, it came from black folks."

Sometimes it played in reverse. Dorothy Brunson: "I grew up where being light and red-haired was a worse problem than being black and female, where black folks say, 'Yeah, white,' and all that. I grew up in an integrated neighborhood in New York City, which had a little bit of everything, so it wasn't that much of a problem there. But black kids pulling your little two-inch pigtails because you're too light, that I suffered. Also I was a very tall twelve-year-old. Probably a foot taller than most people in my class. I was ashamed of my color and ashamed of my red hair, and that I was tall, a bit plump, and had big feet. Those are the things that I had to overcome."

Many other women also mentioned receiving negative messages from friends and sometimes even kin. "You're too dark." "You're too yellow." "You ain't got no color!" "Your hair's too red, too short or too nappy." "You've got a big nose, big lips, and big feet." Or, "Go find the Vaseline and grease your ashy legs."

In Audrey Edwards and Craig K. Polite's *Children of the Dream*, Congresswoman Maxine Waters vividly recalled being the "first dark child in her family," and also remembered that her uncles and his buddies used to sit around talking about how fine yellow women were, and how "the only beautiful black woman was a light, yellow woman."

These kinds of messages made dark-skinned girls question their self-worth, but the remarkable thing is that they rejected the image. Maxine Waters never thought anything was wrong with her. She told Edwards and Polite: "It just made me think something was wrong with them. It made me work harder to prove that I was smarter."

For these sisters, someone was always there to wrap them in approval and love. Addie Wyatt, the future labor leader who grew up in the twenties and thirties, remembered her color being scorned by her own community. "The neighbors used to call me 'the little black one' because all of my brothers and sisters were fair complexioned.

"I would sometimes stick my tongue out at them and say things, and of course if you sassed adults you know what that meant. The adults sometimes would spank you and take you in to your mother. Whenever they said 'your little girl,' my mother would say, 'Which one?' They would say 'the black one.' Well, that was me.

"When I was very young I asked my mother, who was a very fair-complexioned woman, 'Why are the other children fair and I am black?' My mother said, 'Look at your daddy. He is black and I married him because I loved him and look what God did for me. He gave me you, and you know I love you. You are so beautiful because you are black like your daddy.'

"She use to tell me that I was beautiful because she said beauty is what beauty does. I began to believe that as a child. Really, I never thought there was anything wrong about being black. I knew that there were some places we couldn't go and some things that we couldn't do because we were black, but I thought black was all right and I thought black was beautiful because my mother told me that over and over again."

Unita Blackwell got the same kind of loving support in her family: "I wanted to feel pretty, feminine, do what women did. We had white powder. White folks used to have white powder—they didn't even want it. It was real white, like talcum. I would powder up. I had red lipstick on, and white powder on my face. Me being real dark, and those white eyes coming out from under there. That was about all you could see. My family—we all lived in the house together—they laughed and would hug me and say, 'Come on, Miss Little Fast Girl,' which was what my mother called me because I never stopped talking."

Dorothy Brunson, the girl who thought she was too big and too clumsy and too red-haired, learned to love herself just as she was, but it took a while: "When I was immature, I dieted and starved and did all of those foolish things. I guess in my early thirties, I began to realize I wasn't going to have long flowing hair. I realized I'd never get my foot in a size eight. At some point you have to realize that all of the things portrayed as things that make you a better human, or good person, or handsome, or sexy—that you can't be all of that, and that's okay. You are going to wear a size eleven and a half shoe and an eight and a half ring. It is something that you must come to grips with."

The color issue remains unresolved in the African American community. In the sixties and seventies, black was beautiful. Natural hair and natural looks became part of the American mainstream. We celebrated our "color diversity" and praised the multicolored hues of the black community in song, music, and poetry. Sisters were coffee-colored, *latte,* blackberry, honey brown, chocolate, and toffee—and they were all fine. For a brief period, we stopped talking about "good hair" and "fair skin" as the most desirable physical characteristics in men and women.

Unfortunately, the feelings of pride didn't last long and the color issue resurfaced in the eighties and nineties. Today, we are again saturated with stereotypical images of African American women. For the most part they are light, bright, mixed-raced Barbie dolls with hair that blows in the wind; at the other extreme, dark-skinned women are ghetto girls, represented by caricatures such as Sheneneh on the television show *Martin,* played in drag with ratty blond wigs, outrageous fingernails, and huge hoop earrings. Few images fall in between these two extremes. The color thing and the stereotyping thing refuse to die.

Being black was tough. Being dark was rough. But Phenomenal women had even more to learn. They soon discovered that their opportunities were further restricted because they were female. Not surprisingly, several women said they first encountered sexism at home. Gender roles have never been a favorite topic of conversation in the African American community. In fact, sex roles in black families are usually quite rigid. Boys are allowed to run hog-wild, while girls are forced to be responsible. Learning to "keep house" often means cooking, cleaning, and ironing brothers' shirts. Knowing "your place" often means remaining silent when you are ready to speak out.

The common motif of "strength" and "submission" ran like an alternating current through the childhood and teenage years of the future leaders, whether they grew up in the twenties or the sixties. Most said they resented it.

Reverend Willie Barrow, born in Texas in 1924: "I always had high motor skills and I wanted to play with my brothers and with the boys. They kept telling me girls don't do this and girls don't do the other. I wanted to ride horses, and they said girls don't do that. I was bucking that all the time. I would go out and catch the horse myself and ride it. I would just go out there on the field and play ball. I would just butt my way in, and they would let me play."

Some parents, however amazed, seemed to admire their daughter's exploits. Unita Blackwell, born in Mississippi in 1933, said: "I knew I didn't fit. I talked too much and asked too many questions. I used to climb trees and get way up and look out over things. My mother would say, 'What are you doing in that tree?' My aunt used to say, 'That girl has a high mind.'

"I was in a meeting recently with Johnnetta Cole in Atlanta and seventy-five other black southern women leaders. Do you know, all of us can climb trees? None of us quite fit the girl mold when we were little."

It was no different for Shirley Franklin, born in Philadelphia in 1945: "I was expected to jump rope, while boys were riding bikes around the block. They had much more freedom of movement in the neighborhood. In the winter I'd be the only girl playing outside, the only girl in the snowball fight. I got treated differently, both by girls and boys, as a result of that. I went through a period of wanting to reject anything that was feminine. I was trying to figure out how one operates as a black, how one rejects what is feminine, all at the same time."

Most of the women said their awareness of sexism intensified during junior high and high school. Dr. Dolores Cross, former president of the New York State Higher Education Services Corporation, and president of Chicago State University, had this tale to tell about school experiences in the fifties: "I wanted to be a runner, but they didn't stress physical activity for girls. I ran anyway. I wanted to be a cheerleader so I could be close to the football team, but they had only one black female, and you had to be fair complexioned. So I learned to play the clarinet and joined the marching band. I used these skills as a means to an end, to reinforce the feeling that I was special."

Shirley Franklin, who presently wears her hair in a short-cropped natural style: "I cut my hair a little shorter than this when I was thirteen. I remember going to the hairdresser and saying, 'Okay, this is it. I want it all off. I don't want to worry about this anymore.' For me, that was a political statement. I did not want to be judged based on the way I looked. Primarily, that was a reaction to being female and still is."

Pamela Carter, the future attorney general for the state of Indiana, was an athletically talented young teenager. "I ran track. Because I was very fast I was beating the boys. One boy that I beat was the fastest track star on the other team, and his father berated him in front of his friends. We were good friends, and I remember how humiliated he was. His father said he had to run against me until he beat me. Well, I knew that he couldn't, so I let him win. That was the first time. All of this happened within our own race."

Marcia Gillespie: "The gender thing hit me when I was almost thirteen. It was in the Baptist church. One Sunday, the preacher called a girl, not much older than I, about sixteen or so, up in front of the church. He announced that she was pregnant and that she had to beg for the church's forgiveness. I freaked. It was like, 'Wait a minute. This is not fair.' There was no discussion of who got her pregnant. It was the first time I realized that women were scapegoats. The double-standard thing."

While sexism in the African American community combined with some negative color issues, the combination was much more lethal in the mainstream. When and how they faced the "double whammy" depended on when they entered predominantly white environments. Some avoided much of the self-corroding poison until they were grown up and ready to leave home. Those who attended integrated elementary or secondary schools had to deal with it earlier.

In mainstream society racism and sexism were so deeply embedded that they blended together into a thick, seemingly impenetrable barrier. One sister described trying to fight the local high school officials when she was being steered into the home economics curriculum. When her own efforts failed, her mother charged forth. "My mother came to school. 'She's going to have an academic diploma,' she said. They said, 'No, a home economics diploma is the best choice for girls.' " Her mother objected, citing her daughter's intellectual gifts and exceptionally high grades. The administrators took another tack, now claiming that domestic skills were the most useful training for a poor black girl if she hoped to have future employment. "But my mother beat them down," this Phenomenal woman proudly recalled, "till I wound up with both kinds of diplomas."

This kind of double-barreled attack was common, making it hard for the girls to clearly distinguish the primary source of their obstacles. If they managed to deflect one form of discrimination, the other popped up in its place. Often, they said, their mothers held everything together for them. Dorothy Brunson said that all the way through school she was a great reader. "There were pieces that started to take effect and reinforce the positive. I never had a real hard lack of female things. My mother and my aunt were very positive about being black and being female."

Mary Hatwood Futrell's mother and schoolteachers addressed the issues of racism and sexism directly, giving her such a powerful sense of direction that she began to view these barriers as challenges to her grit and ingenuity. "I was raised to be proud of who I was as an individual, as a black person, as a woman. Regardless."

From childhood through adolescence, the startling contrasts between extra attention and racist-sexist barriers went a long way toward explaining why these particular women succeeded in breaking through against the odds.

In early childhood they had already developed a positive self-image and a determination to succeed, long before they began to encounter the vicious, self-eroding effects of racism and sexism. By then they were strong enough to reject any attempt to belittle them. Negative encounters seemed to give them an even stronger sense of purpose. By the time they reached their midteens or late teens, they were already learning to incorporate racial uplift and women's liberation into their personal agendas. Their commitment to civil and human rights was becoming palpable.

Since they had similar developmental experiences, it was to be expected that they would begin to discover similar ways to solve problems. The similarities among them were remarkable. Although they described the process in various ways, they all began to visualize a kind of loosely formed "grid" in their mind's eye. The grid had four interactive chambers, each compartment containing either positive or negative life experiences.

Two positive chambers contained personal and environmental supports. Personal support might include their innate intelligence, educational preparation, family nurturing, spirituality, and a high level of self-esteem. Environmental supports usually included community assets, church, school programs, and new opportunities. It almost always included the community's ongoing struggle for civil rights, a legacy of strength and perseverance, and a heritage of survival and achievement against the odds.

In direct contrast were the two negative chambers, which contained personal and environmental constraints. Personal constraints that might intervene included making poor choices and poor decisions, inability to take advantage of new opportunities, low self-esteem, separation from family, lack of direction, and excessive self-centeredness. They were also aware of the environmental constraints imposed by racism, sexism, economic exploitation, and institutionalized discrimination.

As they matured and tried to move forward in their lives and work, the sex-race obstacles they encountered became more vehement and more complicated. They began to use the grid to process information, interpret their experiences, and help make decisions. Information flowed back and forth among the chambers, a process that many women described as an inner dialogue. They developed a pronounced ability to assess their present situation and, in a holistic way, determine the cause and cure for the current predicament, whatever it was.

Once begun, the grid remained open and free-flowing, providing a framework the women could use to understand the interactive effects of the black female experience as they moved on with their adult lives. Over time, the flexible grid would expand as new life experiences contributed new information.

5

Coming of Age

I was concerned about how I was going to fit into this crazy place. Harvard is not a nurturing environment for anybody. If I had to advise any young person now, it would be to go somewhere else for undergraduate school. Get your head together. Get a sense of self, and then come to graduate school at Harvard. They are, frankly, the best.

—*Fran Farmer*
Former President,
Operation Crossroads Africa

Young adulthood is a turbulent period for all of us, coming on the heels of the challenges of adolescence. According to life cycle theorist Erik Erikson, adolescents are driven by the need to free themselves from parental control and attachments, and to answer the fundamental question: Who am I? When they emerge from the rebellious stage, fragile identities in hand, the next major challenge is young adulthood, the stage when they are forced to find a responsible, productive role and assume adult responsibilities.

Young African American women face the same challenges, but their efforts to find a direction and set their future course are hampered by racist and sexist assumptions about the various roles they are expected to play in both the black and white communities. Sooner or later, Phenomenal women had to find a way to develop their fullest capacities in both environments.

As they left adolescence behind, they considered their options. "Finding a husband" is usually the primary emphasis in black families. Even today, when career options are greater than ever before, young women still feel the pressure of trying to find a mate. How to find a loving, doting spouse is a major theme in conversation, literature, and popular magazines. At times, it would seem that the entire single black female population is *Waiting to Exhale*. And women who remain single for too long are still viewed as suspect.

However, Phenomenal women did not necessarily view the traditional role of wife, mother, and full-time homemaker as a priority. As young women, their lives already went far beyond the domestic sphere. They were too bright, too inquisitive—"junior activists in training." Their circle of interests had grown beyond their immediate and extended families. In their late teens, many were already deeply invested in social causes and in the larger community.

Basically, their choice of which step to take next into adulthood depended largely on the era in which they came of age. Most of the younger women went on to college and graduate school. Most of the older women established themselves in grassroots activism. The experiences of the two age groups were quite different.

The older women often married and in their early twenties bore children, although the traditional role of nurturer and caretaker was seldom completely satisfying. They found many different ways to participate in the larger world. Some preached on street corners, others volunteered for community programs and political action groups. Almost all also held jobs to help support their families.

Prior to the Civil Rights struggle, few jobs awaited black women, particularly in the South. Unita Blackwell recalled: "We had jobs like picking cotton. You might have gotten a job in a laundry. If you had some education you could teach. The most important thing was to learn how to read and write so you could work in a store. Or work in somebody's house if you knew how to read directions. I found myself doing that kind of thing.

"It's not like now, when you get out of school and go to job training. We didn't have that. You just got out of school and if you found something to do, you did it. I worked in houses. I worked in canning plants. I worked in fields. That's how it was."

Unita married soon after graduating from high school in 1951. She did "all this basic kind of thing." Church work inspired her to get involved in local Civil Rights activities. "It wasn't women's groups or other things. For me, it was the church we belonged to. The Civil Rights movement started me to gather myself together. It had a tremendous impact on me. I was about twenty-eight or thirty years old when I got started, because we're talking from 1962. I always knew that it wasn't right to be treated the way we were being treated, and here were people who understood what I'd been feeling all of these many years."

In 1964 Unita joined the Student Nonviolent Coordinating Committee (SNCC), and then the NAACP. "The NAACP was a hidden kind of group to us. We were poor people. We knew about them, but we didn't know how to join them or anything."

Her contacts with other Civil Rights workers grew wider as she showed herself willing to risk her life. She credits northern women's groups, white and black, for coming to her aid when things got rough. "They started coming down to Mississippi in 1965 to get us out of jail. That's how I run into them. We didn't know anything about all these kinds of groups. They would come and talk to us at the jail. They used to call it 'Wednesday in Mississippi.' These women were different. They taught me, and a lot of other people, a lot of what they knew."

Unita was jailed many times. "Sometimes I'd just walk out of the house and get arrested, because my name was in the Commission Report. They started to spot all of us, to make sure we didn't get a job, make sure we didn't get any credit. I didn't get any credit until 1980. Just fighting every step of the way. We sued everything in the state of Mississippi. We had to file lawsuits for housing, lawsuits for just walking down the street. So I was arrested a lot. One time, I was arrested every day for a month. Put in jail, your resources are taken away. We didn't have much anyway. This movement didn't have money. The people didn't have it, we used to not have food to eat. The fine was twelve dollars and fifty cents, but we didn't have the twelve fifty. When the whites and blacks started coming down from the North and from the West, they had some resources, and they got us out."

In 1966 Unita joined the highly respected National Council of Negro Women (NCNW), headed by Dorothy Height, where she found a bountiful group of sisters working hard in the Civil Rights struggle. "That's when I got to know these other kinds of very sophisticated ladies. A lot of learning went on in this, too. Everything was moving fast. We did a lot of things, anything, everything, around the clock. People used to ask me, 'How long you been in politics?' I'd say, 'Oh, this is what I'm in?' "

Like many grassroots activists Unita was initially motivated by urgent need rather than political concepts. "For me it was an absolutely necessary, everyday operation to live. I had no idea that it was called politics. As I look back, people say now, 'You did all that stuff?' You know, we did a lot of things. Then people started calling me names, saying, 'You're an activist; you're an organizer.' All I was was a survivor. I got into this movement to survive, and try to develop some kind of survival for my children and for my husband. That's where I was at."

Unita's extraordinarily creative solutions to problems seemed obvious to her. "The house I lived in, you could look anywhere and look outdoors. It was falling down. So I developed the first home ownership opportunity program in the United States. Out of necessity, out of the hole in my wall."

Soon, Unita's will to survive transcended the needs of her immediate family. She began to direct her efforts toward helping all of Mississippi's disenfranchised citizens. As the Civil Rights movement raged on, its impact widened. Unita Blackwell became one of its most forceful national organizers.

"In 1964 we challenged the seating of the regular Democratic Party from the state of Mississippi, which was all-white, mostly male. See, we didn't know about politics. Ella Baker was the person who talked to us about how to put together the Mississippi Freedom Democratic Party. She was a fantastic woman. Not just because of all the work she did for the NAACP and all the rest of the stuff nobody never knew about. She put all the stuff together for us. There were four of us, Fannie Lou Hamer and Victoria Gray and Annie Devine, and me. My job as the organizer was to make sure that they got down there on the floor. They were the three that were running for the Mississippi House of Representatives in 1965."

That's when Unita knew for sure she was in politics. "The men in my local community looked at me and said, 'Why don't you run for office?' I was getting ready to run for different positions, board supervisor, and so on. So I ran for justice of the peace in 1967. That's the first time I ran for office. I didn't win. We didn't have the votes, we were just getting people registered.

"When we went after things we understood that it was a possibility that we would not win. Mostly my job was to make sure other people ran."

"We did a lot of things in 1964, '65, '66, and '67. Clean on into the seventies. That's when we started seeking another kind of change. We had to start talking about economic development. Economic development *is* the Civil Rights movement, but at the time they saw it as different." Unita remained flexible, and with her usual creative energy, focused on the new target.

"In 1976 I was working for the National Council of Negro Women, and Dorothy Height let us do anything we wanted to. I worked on a lot of different projects. Actually, what it was was creating programs out of your head. Hamer and I were sitting around one day and we said, 'It's time for us to figure out how we're going to sustain ourselves and build leadership in our local communities.'

We wanted to set up a community development center, so we gave it a name and incorporated it. It turned out to be a major organization."

Unita Blackwell came from an ongoing tradition of activist men and women who knew that the advancement and uplift of the community was dependent on their willingness to make a contribution. Political activism born of necessity and creating something out of nothing were her trademarks.

Like Unita Blackwell, Willie Barrow also came of age before the Civil Rights movement and was later transformed by it. Even as a child Willie recognized injustice when she saw it. She started organizing way back when, in the midthirties. "I started on my way to school. I didn't understand why we had to walk and white children had to ride. I organized kids to block the buses and wouldn't let them go by. That was about fifty or sixty children in the road at one time, and that's what happened."

As a teenager Willie started preaching in Sunday school. "It tore the class up. The class started growing and got so big the minister, my father, began to ask, 'What's wrong? How did you get all these young people in this class?' I was just drawing people off the street and bringing them into class. He said, 'Well, Willie is doing something right.'

"I never asked to speak. Wherever I was I just started doing what I could do best, right where I was. I began to hold prayer meetings. We started out with four people and ended up with fifty or sixty people meeting consistently and just praying. We started going to the prisons. Forty or fifty of us would get in cars and go to minister to the prisoners. Then I would speak before the prisoners and they'd get saved. That was a real ministry, and the papers started writing about these young people visiting the prisoners. Then I started having street meetings on the streets. I never asked to preach in anybody's pulpit. That's when I had the call into the ministry, at sixteen."

After Willie Barrow graduated from high school she moved by herself to the West Coast to study for the ministry. It was 1941, at the beginning of World War II. As the nation geared up to produce war materials, blacks and women for the first time had an unprecedented opportunity for jobs. "My folks didn't have any money to send me to the seminary, so I knew I would have to work my way through. I went there on faith and just decided God was going to open up a way. I embroidered bedspreads and sold pillowcases and sheets to people. That made my tuition. But I couldn't pay my rent."

Reverend Barrow said that God led her to the Kaiser Shipyards, where she applied for a job as a welder. She was offered a night job, but she turned it down when she found out it required daytime training, which would conflict with her classes for the ministry.

"I was caught on a limb. I was living in my little room and unable to pay the rent. I went without food for a week and didn't ask anybody for help and I just began to get weaker and weaker. I decided to go back and tell this man that I wanted that job, but I had to go to school during the day.

"I went back and told him that the Lord sent me and that I was hungry and I didn't have a job and I wanted to go to school and the Lord told me that he was going to hire me. He stared at me like I was crazy. I said, again, 'The Lord told me that you were going to hire me.' I filled out an application and he hired me on the spot.

"I still didn't have any food and I had to work two or three weeks till payday. I went by the store nearby my house and got a cart and loaded it up with about a month of food. Then I went up to the counter, and the owner added it up and told me it was about fifty dollars. That's like three hundred dollars now. I said, 'I don't have the money to pay for it. I just got a job and I've been hungry for five days and the Lord told me to come down here and get me some food and if I told you my story you would let me have this food.' I showed him a copy of my job application where I got hired at Kaiser, and I gave him my address. I went right out the door with my food. He never said a word. I didn't see the man till three weeks later, right after I got my paycheck, and I went back down there and gave him his money. He said he had been trying to tell me that I couldn't take those groceries, but he couldn't speak—God locked his mouth. That's when I really knew that God was on my side."

Willie was able to get the night job without having to go to training classes, so she was able to go to school full-time during the day. She went on to organize the first Black Church of God in Portland, Oregon, which became a thriving congregation. She moved on to another seminary in Chicago and eventually finished up her theological studies at the University of Monrovia in Liberia.

In the early sixties, Reverend Willie Barrow joined the Civil Rights movement and became an adviser to Martin Luther King Jr. After King's assassination, she continued working for the movement with the Southern Christian Leadership Conference. The activist spirit led Barrow to PUSH (People United to Serve Humanity), founded by Jesse Jackson in the late sixties. PUSH was demanding equal opportunity for blacks in the larger community and fighting to give control of every aspect of African American life to the black community. Their focus on racial equality was clear.

Reverend Barrow was in the forefront, organizing and leading boycotts against large corporations so that they would recruit, employ, and retain more African Americans in the workforce. She was the guiding force behind making inroads into such industries as construction, auto manufacturing, transportation, and beauty products. She was state coordinator for Coalition Against Hunger in the midseventies.

"I am an organizer, which means having the ability to focus on a goal and then see what it takes and the number of people it takes to bring through that goal. I started off negotiating and didn't know nothing about negotiations, but ended up able to write contracts that lawyers agreed and approved whenever we would draw up a contract, because we never had money to hire lawyers. So I started out putting together black businessmen and women in order to develop black businesses and entrepreneurs."

Willie Barrow and Unita Blackwell represent the older group of contemporary sisters with power who managed to work their way up through the maze of social resistance without the benefit of a traditional university education. Although Reverend Barrow did go on to higher education, she retained that special self-made quality. Both women demonstrated character traits so powerful that they remain common to Phenomenal women of every age: They are hard-working, deeply committed individuals working tirelessly for the collective good. They are activist women who have a clear mandate: Look at the reality. Stick to the truth. Acknowledge something is wrong. Do something to change it. And be creative in your solutions.

Thirty years later, Shirley Franklin described the special ability black female leaders have to come up with creative solutions: "We have had such a hard time in the United States that it gives us an opportunity to be different. We can think different thoughts. We can challenge our own thoughts and each other's thoughts, and not be ostracized because we're stepping out of line."

As the momentum of the Civil Rights movement ebbed, support for grassroots activism also declined. From then on, having a degree became a prerequisite of obtaining any entry-level professional post. Among the younger, college-educated Phenomenal women, some had attended black institutions and others were among the first to attend predominantly white campuses.

This younger group, all born after 1940, was in a new position. In early childhood they experienced the stranglehold of segregation, but they came of age during the great Civil Rights era of the sixties. For these sisters, the move into young adulthood was marked by a dual message: The road ahead is opening, but don't blind yourself to reality. Their experiences with harsh discrimination coupled with the promise of equality gave them an atypical standard by which to steer their course.

Although many were often denied access to education, it has forever been a highly valued commodity in the African American community. Education is viewed as the pathway to knowledge, the road to respectability, and the key to success. Immediately after the Revolutionary War, free blacks in the North began building their educational institutions. Their efforts were impressive, as "special schools for Negroes" were established in Boston, Philadelphia, Trenton and Burlington, New Jersey.

Within the next forty-five years, 259 black schools and colleges were established by twenty different missionary groups and secular organizations. In almost every instance, African Americans themselves had begun the movement for a free school for black youth. Following emancipation, the rush for education swelled. The federal government, through the Bureau of Refugees, Freedmen, and Abandoned Lands, earmarked over $5 million to supplement funds raised by private agencies for teachers' salaries and buildings.

The federal effort had barely gotten under way when the Hayes-Tilden compromise ended the promise of a new South and a new nation. In a close election in 1876 Rutherford B. Hayes appeared to have lost the presidency to Democrat Samuel J. Tilden of New York. The Republicans contested the returns from four states. Dramatic and threatening squabbling dragged on through the winter; finally, in the spring of 1877, a deal was struck: Democrats conceded the presidency to Hayes in exchange for a Republican promise to end the Reconstruction. The rollback of black progress began immediately. Hayes appointed a former Confederate to his cabinet, distributed patronage to moderate southern Democrats, and soon removed the last federal troops from the region. Efforts to obtain equality and full citizenship for African Americans halted. Educational gains were lost and employment opportunities denied. Civil rights and human rights evaporated.

African Americans fought to hold on to the newly established educational institutions in the North and the South. By the turn of the century, more than ten thousand black students had successfully completed undergraduate degrees. Forced segregation throughout the nation resulted in African Americans limiting their educational choices to historical black colleges, located primarily in the South.

There were very few choices for graduate school. For the most part, advanced degrees were the exclusive purview of predominantly white institutions.

Charles Houston, dean of the Howard University Law School, trained a generation of dedicated attorneys to assail the graduate schools of the South. Their first big win came in 1936 when Lloyd Gaines sued the University of Missouri Law School. Gaines won the suit in the state supreme court, and from that benchmark case the larger battle was waged, eventually opening admissions to graduate schools throughout the South.

Sisters fortunate enough to attend college just prior to the Civil Rights explosion overwhelmingly attended the historical black colleges—North Carolina Central, Spelman, Howard, Florida A&T, and Fisk. Although career options for women were still limited, these strong, nurturing environments were tremendously successful in educating African American students. Faculty expectations were high, and graduation rates surpassed those of predominantly white colleges. You went to a black college to succeed, not to fail. Within the protective confines of all-black campuses, students discussed the harsh realties of race and discrimination in the United States. Here, on these campuses, African American students, fed up with the racial injustice, began the student sit-in movement in the early sixties.

Some sisters took a different collegiate route, becoming among the first to take advantage of new opportunities resulting from the Civil Rights struggle. They were part of the crossover generation: Some integrated high schools, others colleges, and others graduate schools.

In speaking of their experiences on predominantly white campuses, sisters seldom conjured up nostalgic images of "ivy halls" and green pastures. In many cases, they found these environments hostile and resistant.

Josephine D. Davis pursued a degree in mathematics at Spelman College. Later, she attended Notre Dame and Rutgers Universities for graduate degrees. Deborah Prothrow-Stith also attended Spelman College, but later received her medical degree from Harvard. Shirley

Franklin went to Howard, then entered graduate school at the University of Pennsylvania.

By the seventies, the trend was moving steadily toward enrollment on white campuses. (The majority of black students today are now enrolled in predominantly white institutions at both graduate and undergraduate levels.) Maxine Waters, who returned to college in the sixties, received her degree in sociology at UCLA. Cynthia McKinney graduated from the University of Southern California. Pamela Carter pursued social work and prelaw at the University of Detroit; and Marcia Gillespie majored in American studies at Lake Forest College.

Black students enrolling on white campuses were coldly received by faculty and students, and it took courage to withstand the frosty atmosphere. Many black women were told they didn't belong in college. On campuses where some African American students were admitted under Equal Opportunity and affirmative action programs, assumptions were made about the academic qualifications of all black students.

Some of the sisters said that faculty members appeared shocked when they used correct English, displayed critical thinking skills, and expressed informed opinions. Because of their whites-only experience, white professors assumed that their bright black students were exceptions, and treated them almost as "honorary whites." Maintaining one's identity was difficult, but essential. Black women entering universities were seeking advancement opportunities, not transformation into Oreo cookies. No one wanted to become, in the words of our grandmothers, "educated fools."

The major task of educated black females was to develop a careful balancing act that allowed them to be effective in the predominantly white arena, without surrendering their racial identity and cultural integrity. To do this, it was important to find ways to maintain their connections to their communities.

Shirley Franklin, who grew up to become the chief administrative officer for the city of Atlanta, had spent her early childhood in the bosom of a nurturing black community in Philadelphia, where she participated in many social organizations. "I was in Jack and Jill, and young people's activities in NAACP. Clubs can be a way of identifying with people who are like you or that you aspire to be like. I had access to a church that I felt had the right perspective that interested me."

As a result of de facto residential segregation in Philadelphia, Shirley attended pseudosegregated elementary and junior high schools. Then, in the early sixties, she was selected to enter Philadelphia's Girls High, a barely integrated public school for gifted teenage girls, with an all-white female faculty. This was the first time she was in a predominantly white environment.

"I remember I was asked to model for the art classes. I sometimes wore an Indian sari, almost as if they were trying to give me a different identity. It made me a little uncomfortable, but not enough to rebel. I knew that some people wanted to make me and the other black girls in the class an exception. I didn't want to be an exception all the time. You just want to be one of the girls in the class."

Shirley realized that certain very high achievers in her school had access to resources she didn't have. "They lived near school or their mothers picked them up after school. They went to tutorial services, they always had supplemental reading, and someone to instruct them. I was a good student, but I did it on my own. I always wished that I had more to lean on, so that I could get 150 percent out of the course instead of just 95 percent. I'm not talking about grades, I'm talking about an insight, a point of view."

Shirley saw her teachers, all of whom had advanced degrees, as role models and leaders. Many were active in social causes of the time, which were largely antiwar, "ban the bomb" issues. But black history was absent from the curriculum. She had to find a way to expand her opportunities, and also educate herself about her own historical and cultural background. In that process, she fine-tuned the art of making something out of nothing.

"I had to travel about an hour and a half each way to school on public transportation through the central part of Philadelphia. On the way home I used to stop downtown and go to the library five days a week. Sometimes I would come back down on Saturdays, too. In my browsing there I found Albert Lee Rufuley's book *Let My People Go*. From reading Rufuley, I realized that it wasn't just in the United States that black people had a burden to bear. That was my first interest in South Africa."

Shirley stayed closely tied to her community through her volunteer activities. "I worked in a children's hospital and at Temple University Hospital. These are things I sought out myself, for the same reason I went to the library and to the art museum. It was difficult to find out who I was and what I wanted to be about. I found if I worked with people who were in fairly desperate situations, with crisis in their lives, I didn't focus so much on myself. My mother was also very active in the community, but I don't remember her ever insisting that I do anything. Most of the time these were things I sought out on my own."

For the most part, Shirley remembers Girls High as a positive educational experience. In the long run, the obstacles that she encountered in a white environment motivated her to try harder. "On the one hand, I was not in an environment that had a systematic way of exposing me to black leadership; on the other, it wasn't so limiting that there weren't opportunities there."

Shirley was very active in student government and student affairs. She was treasurer of her class, and served in half a dozen clubs in a variety of positions. "When I was leaving Girls High I remember a young white friend said she expected great things from me. I was astounded, because it never dawned on me that I was anything other than average."

By the time Shirley graduated from Girls High she had an intense desire to change the world. "I wanted to see beyond the here and now of my life. I wanted to look at the world in a way that you could turn it upside down. I specifically wanted to be part of the group that overthrew the South African government."

After her high school experience, Shirley would have chosen an integrated women's college for herself. Her mother, however, encouraged her to "come back to reality." Shirley went to Howard and was deeply involved in the faculty and student movements of the sixties. Shirley earned a bachelor of arts in sociology, with a double minor in African studies and psychology. She chose the University of Pennsylvania for graduate school, returning once again to a predominantly white environment.

When Shirley entered the graduate school of sociology at the University of Pennsylvania in 1967, she cast around for advice and mentoring and found no black professors. The key to success for any postgraduate, particularly for doctoral candidates, is based on finding a mentor to help you through. Only a few of the women who had attended graduate school said they were fortunate enough to find black professors to mentor them.

Shirley Franklin said, "I found graduate school fairly racist in its orientation toward sociology. You have 150 books in a bibliography on a course about urban sociology and the only black author quoted is a novelist. James Baldwin is wonderful, but he is not W. E. B. Du Bois. All of the work about Puerto Ricans was by white males. It was ridiculous. I had come from Howard and I knew that black people could read and write and publish. I was never successful in influencing change in the graduate school. We did read Frantz Fanon in one of my courses. There were about five or six black students in the class, and the professor felt he should be at Oxford instead of Penn. He opened up to the black students, wanting our input. I remember clamming up and refusing to say a word because I knew he wanted my point of view in order to publish himself. As I see it now, those were fairly insignificant rebellions against the system.

"Basically, I defined an area where I could achieve and make a contribution, and I went for it. I accepted the status quo. I think that's largely because I didn't have any concrete role models. I finally became disgusted with graduate school, and decided I wouldn't attend classes. I just showed up at the finals and did fairly well. This infuriated some of my teachers. But I didn't try to disrupt anyone else's participation, I just limited my own.

"I had a big problem in my statistics course. It's not anything unusual to teach yourself statistics. But my professor changed the scoring system on the final, which lowered my grade from an *A* to a *B*+. I had spent the majority of my time on the questions that would have gotten me the *A*. I went to see him to challenge the change in scoring. Now, he hadn't seen me since September, and this is in May. The first thing out of his mouth was, 'I think you've done very well, considering your background.' I remembered he came from an immigrant family. And I said, 'I'll tell you about my background, and let's see about yours.' Needless to say, he didn't change my grade."

Shirley developed a reputation as a troublemaker, which made finding a mentor even more difficult. "I sought out a white professor of political sociology and took a reading course with him. Just the two of us. After the second or third week, I remember he said, 'Everybody's been talking about you. You're not so bad.' One-on-one, we worked very well."

Shirley walked out of her master's finals because she refused to answer several questions that she considered to be racist, but she earned enough credits to graduate. After several years of struggling to find a comfortable place in predominantly white environments, she managed to hold her graduate degree in one hand, and an intact racial and cultural identity in the other.

About the same time, farther west, another future power broker was finding her identity and establishing her direction. Her memories of her educational experiences in predominantly white institutions were more positive. Apparently, Indianapolis was the right place to be in the fifties. Pamela Carter, future attorney general of the state of Indiana: "If I can say it, it was an absolutely perfect environment for a young person to grow up in. We lived in the only community in the United States where they allowed African Americans to build their own homes. My father was a part of this grand experiment. He built one of the homes in this model neighborhood, and my childhood and adolescence in that environment was unique. It was all African American.

"Not too far from there we also had projects, which were also the first of their kind in the nation. I don't know if people realize that Indiana tends to be a vanguard state, even though it is conservative. That was my world through eighth grade."

Pamela's first taste of integration had taken place at the age of eight in a Catholic Youth camp. Her second foray was attending a predominantly white all-girls Catholic high school. "I didn't come out of junior high with a lot of deficits, because I was well prepared academically and I had great self-esteem. I hit the ground running and did well in school. I never had to evaluate myself poorly in comparison with white students.

"People can say what they want, but those nuns ran a tight ship. They cared very much for us, and it was probably the most wonderful four years I ever spent. It was a very nurturing, but exacting and demanding environment. As I think back, they were good role models. We had a female principal, and at the time they thought they might have to close the school. The principal had gone to all the traditional areas to get money and couldn't. Then she came to the students and said, 'This wonderful institution, after over one hundred years, will close unless you can raise *x*-number of dollars.'

"We did it. She empowered all of us, and we raised double the amount of money we needed. She was exerting leadership in nontraditional ways. It really became our school. It was an extraordinary experience."

After graduation, Pamela went on to the University of Detroit, a small Jesuit Catholic college with a large number of African American students. "I was very active in the Civil Rights movement. I was majoring in social work and prelaw. I was in VISTA. I worked in Cabrini Green Projects and at the Democratic National Convention. I was involved in everything. It was an invigorating period for me."

When Pamela graduated from the university in 1971, she decided to pursue a graduate degree in social work from the University of Michigan. "At that time, social work was a profession that was held in high esteem, and the University of Michigan was number one. There was a lot of internal pride there. We had very good and committed professors, and I learned a lot. We were very much engaged in what was going on. It was a positive experience for higher education." Because she had grown up and come of age while living in a solid black community, Pamela never had any difficulty hanging on to her cultural identity in college.

Pamela was working as a social worker when she looked out and discovered new opportunities opening up. Like other college-educated women of that period, sisters were beginning to seek professions other than teaching, nursing, and social work. These women were again traveling unchartered paths. They, too, had to accept the role of trailblazers, shattering stereotypical images of the limited abilities of blacks and women. Pamela decided to go on to law school at Indiana University. The chances of any African American student finding an African American role model in law or medicine were slim to none.

At Indiana University race and sex reemerged as dominant issues in Pamela's life. "Not only was the environment not nurturing, but people questioned whether you should even be there." Pamela found no mentors in law school. She stayed close to her family and relied on her parents to guide her development. African American history and experience in the Civil Rights movement taught her the rest. She had marched with Martin Luther King Jr. back in the 1960s and continued to rely on figures from history for inspiration. She was particularly moved by Harriet Tubman's story. "She was always so successful in getting people through the Underground Railroad. She had nothing, but yet she was able to exact so much from life and give so much back. She was dismissed, but yet she prevailed. Nothing came easy. I've always been so intrigued by that." Thus, like Shirley Franklin, Pamela came out with excellent professional credentials and her cultural identity fully intact.

In 1962 Marcia Gillespie's academic achievements in high school were rewarded with a four-year scholarship from the National Scholarship Service and Fund for Negro Students. She left the community comfort of Long Island to attend Lake Forest College in Illinois. Like Pamela, she found no black female role models, but she was fortunate to find two white male mentors, Dr. John G. Sproat and Dr. Nathan J. Huggins. "They goaded me, you know, the whole nine yards. But they both affirmed that 'you can do this.' I decided to major in American studies because I liked history. It wasn't because I had an idea of what I wanted to do. I didn't have a clue. And to be real honest, I graduated still not quite clear. I thought, maybe I'll work, then go to graduate school, and maybe end up teaching American studies."

In the thirty-plus years since the initiation of the black student protest movement, the faculty picture has changed somewhat. Today, blacks represent 4 percent of the overall faculty, and women 22 percent. However, most are teaching in junior and four-year colleges, rather than the more prestigious doctoral-granting research institutions.

Throughout these years black educational achievement has been accompanied by the malicious racism of William Shockley, Arthur R. Jensen, and more recently Charles Murray, who masqueraded as proven "science" their theories that intelligence was transmitted genetically. Their contention that it is a waste of money to try to educate African Americans contributes to the ethnic and racial divisions on many campuses today. The legitimacy of African American students continues to be challenged, and new debate over affirmative action has become an acceptable way to obscure racist beliefs.

This is the primary reason why black students at Rutgers University exploded over the "genetic inferiority" comments made by their president, Dr. Francis Lawrence. They had believed that their generation had outlived racist assaults on their intelligence. They expected that faculty, especially their president, knew that the somewhat lower test scores and grade averages of some (but by no means all) black students reflected the tests' cultural and racial biases, as well as the historic exclusion of black students from early educational opportunities. The Rutgers students were horrified to learn that old pseudoscientific theories claiming that intelligence was genetically inherited were alive and well.

Many highly distinguished African American students and faculty are, once again, being looked on as if they are in on a free pass. Malcolm X once questioned an audience on how white America views black achievement. "What's a black man with a Ph.D?" he asked. The answer, "A nigger."

The challenge for all African American youth is finding a center—a strong self-identity in contrasting and often conflicting environments. Phenomenal women had developed strong personal identities from childhood, which made them immune to new assaults on their character and dignity as they came of age. Whenever new environments proved too corrosive, they periodically returned home to their families and communities from whence their strength originally came to have their batteries recharged.

No matter where they went, or when, the future leaders retained their cultural ties. Josephine Davis: "If you don't ground yourself in who you are and be proud of that, you'll always be floating between two cultures. You have to be centered first. Know something about yourself. Then look carefully at the landscape. Think ahead."

Josephine, whose image of Africans had been warped by Tarzan movies, found her own center on a trip to Africa as part of a summer enrichment program sponsored by Operation Crossroads Africa when she was nineteen. This proved to be a defining moment for her. "I had read about bloodletting and drinking blood. Africans lived as nomads. I came to find out that, to the contrary, they were the most beautiful people. Even though they lived in cow-dung homes, they were crisp and they were clean. I came to understand why they live as they do. Because of the conditions, everything becomes justifiable. Like *Dances with Wolves,* I saw it through their eyes. It was another person's culture. It made me feel proud that I was black. From then on, I was on a mission to help people realize what had happened to us, what had happened to our heritage. I wanted people to rediscover the African in us."

Young Phenomenal sisters were also a community of joiners: They joined social, political, and national service organizations in droves: Delta Sigma Theta, Alpha Kappa Alpha, and Zeta Phi Beta; the Student Nonviolent Coordinating Committee, the National Association for the Advancement of Colored People; and Volunteers in Service to America. Many of these organizations interfaced with a wide variety of other organizations, some of which represented their adversaries. Through these multidimensional experiences they eventually were able to feel comfortable in every kind of environment. Their new comfort level was derived from education, maintaining close ties to family and community, participating actively in varied experiences, and natural maturing—simply adjusting to their own personas. Above all, it came from a powerful sense of personal identity and belief in themselves.

6

A Hard Road Up

I'm an affirmative action baby. They want to classify affirmative action people as being less than qualified. We have to say, proudly, 'Yes, we are affirmative action, but we are also qualified.'

—*Congresswoman Cynthia McKinney (D-Ga.)*

By the seventies and early eighties, African American women were earning college and advanced degrees in unprecedented numbers. For the first time in history, African American women had an opportunity to set foot on the first rung of the power ladder in business, politics, education, and government. Most of these women were fully aware that their success derived from a long and proud heritage. Mary Hatwood Futrell, former president of the National Education Association and currently dean of the School of Education at George Washington University, is eloquent on the subject:

"If someone had not fought for equal education opportunities, to desegregate the schools, and establish programs to provide an education for black children and for women, I would not be seated here today. If someone had not fought for voting rights, I would not be here today. If someone had not fought for fair housing, I would not be able to live where I live today. If someone had not fought for rights for women, I would not be here today. I am here because black people stood up and fought. Because poor people that I don't even know stood up and fought. When Martin Luther King Jr. was out there putting his life on the line every day, he didn't know me. When Sojourner Truth stood up and said, 'Ain't I a woman,' she didn't know me. But I am their beneficiary."

Paula Banks, president of the Sears Roebuck Foundation, was hired as a trainee by Sears Roebuck after her mother saw a minority recruitment ad in the paper in 1972, when memories of urban rebellions were still fresh in everyone's minds. "I am absolutely a beneficiary of Civil Rights legislation, equal opportunity, affirmative action, and all programs like that. Sears would not have had a minority training program if they hadn't been afraid the stores would get burned down if they didn't.

"Philosophically, Sears believes in doing the right thing, but the bottom line is that from a business standpoint, you want to do what makes sense, what is prudent. When they're burning things down, you don't want your stuff to be burned down, too. So it is pragmatic to do the right thing.

"Yes, I am a 'first black,' and certainly a 'first female.' I was the first black woman to be the Equal Opportunity director for the company in a twelve-state area. I was the only black person to this date to be on the employee relations–labor relations board. I was the first black woman to be a human resources manager.

"If it hadn't been for some strong African American men, fighting men, many of whom are still around paving the way—I wouldn't be here today."

Shirley Franklin, the former chief managing director of the city of Atlanta, added: "No question about it. I would not be in this position if it were not for the dedication of thousands of people all over this country, black and white, predominantly black, to the Civil Rights movement in the fifties and sixties. A lot was started even before then—in the thirties, longer ago than that. We resisted oppression from the time we were captured and from the time we came over. We resisted in different ways. But there is no question that I am here largely because of the opportunities that are afforded through electoral politics. I am a direct beneficiary and my children are direct beneficiaries."

It had been a long road. Racism was born during a period of unrestricted growth and expansion in the American colonies. Believing that people of color were inherently inferior was a convenient excuse to maintain and exploit cheap labor. Revolutionary cries for independence did not address the contradictory presence of enslaved human beings, or the denial of fundamental rights to Native Americans. As a result, for two hundred more years millions of American citizens continued to be denied opportunity, creating sharp conflict between the nation's stated beliefs and its actual practices. Several hard-won attempts had been made to redress these wrongs, but each had been successfully defeated.

Even white abolitionist groups fighting for the emancipation of enslaved African Americans were themselves fundamentally racist. Though they thought slavery was evil, they never saw blacks as equals.

The Civil War promised freedom and equality for all Americans. The Civil Rights amendments (the Thirteenth and Fourteenth Amendments), ratified in 1865 and 1868, established that African Americans were free people entitled to all rights of citizenship and due process. In 1870, the Fifteenth Amendment gave the vote to black men. The Freedmen's Bureau, a hundred-year-old precursor to affirmative action, attempted to redress past injustices by redistributing confiscated and abandoned lands, providing funds for education, and helping to negotiate employment contracts for newly emancipated African Americans. None lasted for very long.

The Civil Rights Act of 1875, while providing some additional protection, also invalidated statutes that had prohibited racial discrimination by innkeepers, common carriers, and places of amusement. But when Republican Rutherford B. Hayes managed to overturn Samuel J. Tilden in the presidential election of 1876, he appeased southern Democrats by pulling the last federal troops out of the region. Immediately de jure and de facto Jim Crow laws sprang up all over the country, and terrorist groups brutally attacked and murdered black people trying to exercise their legal rights.

In *When and Where I Enter,* Paula Giddings describes Ida B. Wells-Barnett, from Holly Springs, Mississippi, as an outspoken warrior against injustice. In 1884, Wells-Barnett was among the first to sue the railroads over discriminatory services. Her lower-court victory was overturned, but she kept up the attack by writing articles for the black press.

Journalism became her sword. When three friends were lynched, Wells-Barnett exposed the atrocities by raising a noisy, militant voice in her column in *Memphis Free Speech,* which she wrote under the pen name "Iola." She successfully rallied blacks to boycott white businesses and was forced to flee the South to escape threats on her life. She continued her campaign in New York.

Despite her firebrand magnetism Wells-Barnett never held a national leadership position in the civil rights struggle. Black organizations considered her behavior "inflexible" and "unsuitable." Ironically, these same words are used to describe many contemporary powerful sisters, whose blunt style grates on the polished surface of the establishment.

Events continued to spiral downward. In a case involving the segregation of railroad passengers, the Supreme Court held that "separate but equal" public facilities did not violate the Constitution. The disastrous *Plessy* v. *Ferguson* decision of 1896 legitimized society's de facto Jim Crow structure, upholding state laws that segregated blacks in railroads, trolley cars, rest rooms, hospitals, parks, sports arenas, theaters, housing, and even cemeteries. These laws remained firm throughout the first half of the twentieth century, and overt and covert racial exclusion was practiced in most areas of the United States.

From the beginning, the black struggle for equality was closely intertwined with the struggle for women's rights. A few women pioneered for equal rights in revolutionary days, but not until the abolitionist movement did large numbers fully begin to recognize their own differential, inferior status.

The historical rift between black and white women was born in all-female antislavery societies, which acted as auxiliaries to the more powerful all-male organizations. One group of white women in New York agreed to admit black women to their abolitionist society, then immediately voted to dissolve the organization. Elsewhere, white societies forced black women members to sit in separate sections in the meeting halls.

In a few organizations black and white women did work together freely. In Philadelphia, black women assumed some of the leadership roles, forging bonds within and between disparate groups and building a network of personal and professional friendships. This early demonstration of consensus building is still evident in the way powerful black women do business today.

In cities where racism was intractable, black women formed their own abolitionist societies. Their ability to push two conflicting movements forward simultaneously became a distinct feature of their leadership.

When middle- and upper-class white women began to rally for equal treatment, black women hoped that their vision would include all women. It didn't. In her acclaimed work *Terrible Honesty*, Ann Douglas describes how the suffrage movement actually widened the chasm between black and white women.

In 1867, Susan B. Anthony and Elizabeth Cady Stanton, editor of the *Woman's Bible*, joined forces with George Train, a wealthy supporter whose public motto was "women first, and Negro last." Stanton and Anthony refused to lobby for the Fifteenth Amendment, which guaranteed the vote to black men, on the grounds that it did not include female suffrage. By contrast, most black women supported the Fifteenth Amendment. The amendment passed and was ratified in 1870.

The year of the *Plessy* v. *Ferguson* decision, Josephine St. Pierre Ruffin, a friend of Stanton and Anthony, and editor of the first black women's newspaper, *Woman's Era*, helped found the National Association of Colored Women (NACW). NACW's motto, "Lifting As We Climb," dramatized the double burden carried by African American women. On every level, the gap between black women and white women around the turn of the century was wider than the gap between white women and white men.

With enslavement only a few years in the past, those few black women in the middle class remained closely bound to their sisters below them. When Ida B.Wells-Barnett, for example, was accused of having socialist sympathies, her more conservative sisters still supported her in protesting lynching and the incessant infractions of Negro rights.

Black women as a whole also stood in support of black men. After the Fifteenth Amendment passed, black men returned the favor by lobbying for woman suffrage.

Even as they did so, the National American Woman Suffrage Association (NAWSA) assured its foes that if women were given the vote, white women would outnumber, and outvote, male and female black voters combined. In effect, they promised that women suffrage would make African American disenfranchisement permanent. New laws were passed to keep black men out of the voting booths, including property requirements, poll tax, and clever manipulation of the new primary system of national elections. Even Jane Addams, pioneer social work activist and an early member of the NAACP, agreed to support Theodore Roosevelt's Progressive Party in 1912 when it upheld the idea of woman suffrage but refused to include a Negro-rights plan in its platform.

Carrie Chapman Catt, former schoolteacher and president of NAWSA, favored a steep literacy requirement that would disqualify the majority of blacks from voting. She publicized her opinion, knowing that her views would appeal to President Woodrow Wilson. Although Wilson was not friendly to the suffrage cause, Catt's strategy paid off. In 1917, Wilson backed suffrage in exchange for Catt's public support for his decision to bring America into the war.

These maneuverings were conducted in plain view: In 1899 the national suffrage convention had turned down a resolution put forth by black women opposing Jim Crow cars on the railroads. In 1913, white suffragists had asked their black colleagues not to march with them in the suffrage parade in Washington. And in 1919, NAWSA refused to accept a group of the Colored Negro Women's Clubs as members.

But throughout, black women continued to support women's suffrage. When America entered the war, thousands of women took their men's places in the labor force, not only in offices, but also in industrial enterprises like steel production and auto manufacturing. NAWSA's membership doubled, going from two million to four million, and suffrage leaders expanded the Red Cross and sat on prestigious national war commissions.

In 1920, the suffrage amendment went to the states for approval. Women won the vote and quite suddenly lost interest in the political process. The feminist movement retreated from the national scene as the new voters returned to their domestic roles and proceeded to vote pretty much as their men did.

Those remaining in the old suffrage organization were absorbed into the women's peace movement. Again, black women were unwelcome. When the International Council of Women for Peace met in April of 1925, black delegates walked out after they discovered that the seating arrangements were segregated. The National Association of Colored Women continued to fight lynchings throughout the twenties with little help from the large white women's organizations.

Women again experienced a significant change in status during World War II when the need for additional industrial "manpower" required them to leave home once more and enter the workforce. Their experiences did not generate a new feminist movement. Following victory, a domestic propaganda campaign launched by government and industry convinced most women to resume their domestic roles, although some, usually from necessity, found other jobs.

Ironically, the feminist movement did not come alive again until it tailed into the power stream of the modern-day Civil Rights movement. Rosa Parks's refusal to move to the back of the bus after a long day's work symbolized the unique status of black women: an underemployed, overworked, exploited population carrying the burden of both race and sex.

Toward the end of the sixties, the nation's two most powerful movements to fight injustices—the Civil Rights–Black Power and women's movements—converged.

Things got even more complicated when the impassioned Black Power movement erupted into the mix. An underlying conflict between black men and women flared in response to the question, "Who shall lead?" Sexism was a dominant theme. In two extreme examples, SNCC leader Stokely Carmichael told women that their position in the protest movement was "prone," and Black Panther Eldridge Cleaver advocated rape as a form of protest. Cleaver's main target was white women, but he recommended "practicing" on black women. Even with these moments of temporary lunacy, however, most sisters continued to feel that the African American community, including most brothers, had their backs.

The Civil Rights movement awakened the whole country to the entrenched injustices present in employment and educational opportunities. The words *affirmative action* were first uttered by President John F. Kennedy in Executive Order 10925. The intent was clear: The nation would take aggressive action to overcome years of denied opportunity to blacks and other people of color. The policy began to take shape during the debates on the Civil Rights Act of 1964. Affirmative action was presented as more than an attempt to redress three hundred years of rampant race and sex discrimination. By insuring healthy diversity in labor and management, affirmative action was intended to make companies and institutions more responsive to public needs, which ultimately would benefit the whole society. While this effort to guarantee employment and educational opportunities for all Americans was morally and legally sound, not every politician was in favor of the plan. In an effort to defeat the bill in the legislature, "women" were added as a protected group. To the surprise of some members of Congress, the bill passed, and for the first time in history, white males were not guaranteed an automatic leg up. They didn't like it.

White women immediately made the greatest gains. Other groups—Native Americans, Asian Americans, first-generation Spanish-speaking Americans from the Caribbean and South America—also benefited. Sisters also made important social, political, and economic gains.

Affirmative action was never intended to be reverse discrimination nor, in the majority of cases, did it play out that way. The affirmative action guidelines in some organizations did permit awarding jobs, contracts, or promotions to qualified individuals and to companies who hired less experienced individuals and companies who hired individuals who were a particular color or sex. Some even gave jobs to individuals who were less qualified. However, these occurrences were the exception rather than the rule. In most cases, choices had to be made among many qualified people applying for the same position. Those choices got considerably tougher as the job market began to shrink in the late eighties. A recent job search at Richard Stockton College generated more than a hundred qualified applicants—fifteen women and eighty-five men—for a single position. A woman was hired. Were all eighty-five men victims of reverse discrimination because a woman got the job?

In any case, the final choice among job applicants has never been based on the concept that the most meritorious individual gets the job. Consider the unlikely people chosen for some top jobs. How did Frank Rizzo become the mayor of Philadelphia? How did Clarence Thomas make it to the Supreme Court? Subjectivity is part of any selection process, and many factors determine the mix of final job candidates. It is precisely because the final mix repeatedly excluded people of color and women that affirmative action programs were created in the first place.

To stop affirmative action now only means that all of our children and grandchildren will have to confront the old issues of inequality down the line. Certainly, abuses should be eliminated, but as grandmomma used to say, "You don't throw out the baby with the bathwater!"

Affirmative action has helped many black women get off the ground when they hadn't been able to before. In some areas their achievement appears to surpass that of black males. (In those instances, black men and white men tend to complain that black women were hired as a "two-for-one" affirmative action gain.)

For the most part, however, sisters are far from achieving social, economic, and political parity. Those who have managed to work their way up are standing on the most tenuous grounds, still in the midst of a serious struggle that threatens to overwhelm them. They know that the road behind and beyond is still cluttered with barriers of racism, sexism, and classism. The stories they tell of the difficulties they encountered in their early careers show that separating one "ism" from another may be difficult, but ignoring them can be fatal to one's future.

The sisters who started their careers in primarily black organizations usually encountered sexism first. Even in the loving, supportive environment of PUSH, a female-dominated organization, gender was an important issue. Top leadership positions were occupied by men only. Reverend Willie Barrow began as a PUSH organizer and slowly worked her way up, doing every impossible job that came into her hands, and getting remarkable results. "Reverend Jackson didn't quite understand my growth and development. All along the way, he tried to place men in front of me, even though I had achieved. He assumed that black men needed to be leaders, and he liked brothers taking the leadership positions. But when it came to defining and initiating his new programs, the men didn't like the heavy responsibility."

Willie Barrow argued that she shouldn't have to train the brothers for jobs that she was perfectly capable of doing herself. "Reverend Jackson finally said, 'I've got to get someone, man or woman, who will produce because production is the bottom line.' Women always produce. They work twice as hard."

As she made her way up the power ladder at PUSH, Reverend Barrow needed to make sure that her peers and colleagues understood her role. "I said, 'Now, Reverend Jackson, you better send a letter out telling these ministers who don't like women that I'm coming to see them and they will either meet with me or nobody.' I demanded that should happen.

"Once I was in the door, they knew I could deliver. Even though they'd knock me across the head and reject me, I was still nice and sweet and accommodating. I'd get right back to my point and move on."

Like Willie Barrow, other Phenomenal women were also willing to start with almost any job that had prospects, and take on any task that needed doing. No matter what the job was, they knew their performance had to be superlative. Mary Hatwood Futrell described the pressure they were under: "Anyone who hopes to reach a top position has to be super good. But for a minority to get there, we have to be super, super good."

As they moved into their first jobs, the search for mentors became more difficult than ever. In the absence of women or African Americans in senior positions, many cautiously formed ties with white males.

Paula Banks started her career as a management trainer at Sears Roebuck. "White males did not start out particularly enamored with me. They usually said, 'If I have to accept this plight, I will take you.' Then they would do back flips, saying, 'My God, I didn't know you had this kind of talent.' My challenge was to convince them that I was not an exception. 'Open your eyes! There are talented black people all around you.' "

When Roberta Palm Bradley began her climb in the utility industry she encountered the same reality: a dearth of women, black or white, in leadership positions. Many of her mentors were white males. However, she also said that African American males who had joined the corporation before her helped her navigate the maze of corporate politics.

African American women also began to form professional relationships with their white female peers. Without a career plan, Marcia Gillespie accidentally fell into journalism. At the time, affirmative action was beginning to make an impression on corporate America, and Time, Inc., was searching for minorities to help diversify their predominantly white male staff. Marcia was hired as a researcher, practically the only nonclerical job that any woman was allowed to fill in the company. Trying to find a black female role model, Marcia found Beatrice Doby instead. Beatrice, then head of the research department, impressed twenty-one-year-old Marcia because she was "so cool."

Marcia's choice was a good one. Whenever she needed help answering the myriad questions generated by her new position, she reached for the phone to call her department's top boss, and Beatrice was there to help her.

By contrast, many African American women who developed compatible working relationships with white sisters felt that their new bonds were weakly forged. When the chips were down, most black women expected their white female colleagues to line up on the side of the status quo. Their generalized uneasiness in these relationships was a sore spot that stemmed from the long history of past betrayals, which had been passed down through several generations of African American women.

While Marcia Gillespie continued to make friends at Time, Inc., she also realized her gender and race barred her from the power track. Marcia was still a fledgling journalist when she was tapped to become editor in chief of *Essence,* the first popular magazine meant solely for sisters. While *Ebony, Jet,* and *Sepia* provided African Americans with the inside scoop on the world of the black middle class, their coverage of the contemporary experiences of black women was incomplete. *Essence* took sisters on a journey where they had never traveled before.

Founded in 1970 by four young black men who understood business marketing, *Essence* was geared toward young, socially conscious black women whose spirits had been buoyed by the Civil Rights and Black Power movements. Today, *Essence* is a megapower in the communications industry. Its high-profile editor in chief, Susan L. Taylor, keeps the magazine on the cutting edge of social issues that impact black women, the black community, and the entire nation. Susan has guided the expansion of Essence Communications, Inc., into television and concert productions, making the company a national model for publishing enterprises. Susan L. Taylor is highly regarded as one of the most powerful black female role models in America.

But back in the early seventies, few envisioned such an American success story. Twenty-seven-year-old Marcia Gillespie brought a youthful exuberance to the risky venture. With no professional peer group and no network of sisters in similar positions, she had to figure out how to do the job on her own.

Under Marcia's hand, *Essence* became an information-filled national magazine for and about African American women, a magazine of real substance. Every month, each new issue fell into eager, waiting hands. *Essence* celebrated the achievements and nurtured the hearts of young sisters. Marcia's monthly column, "Getting Down," provided a provocative essay that always seemed to capture women's deepest emotions. In every colorful hue and texture, *Essence* proclaimed the beauty of African American women, and provided them with direction and a sense of national identity when none other existed. Ultimately, *Essence* became the premier journal for all black women, attracting a broad-based readership of young and old, single and married, professional, stay-at-home, and hard-working everyday sisters.

As Marcia guided the magazine through its formative years, she certainly encountered many conflict-filled days at the office. For the most part, however, *Essence* was a supportive environment where she was able to develop her editorial style. She dedicated herself to the highest standard of performance and, in so doing, became a role model for millions of black women.

At times, it was extraordinarily difficult. "I don't leap over tall buildings," she said, "and I don't want to, but sisters do bring strength to these new positions of power. We also bring a kind of centeredness. I am not so naive to think that sexism is going to disappear in a minute, any more than I think that racism is, but we have been honed in the struggle. That makes you less likely to be thrown by any little wind that happens to come along. You have had to endure in the gale force."

Like all of her older Phenomenal sisters, Marcia knew that she stood "on the shoulders of all those sisters and brothers who traveled before me. I got my college education from scholarships because of Civil Rights. I got my job at Time, Inc., because of the Civil Rights movement and because the 'fires next time' were burning in the streets of American cities. There would not have been an *Essence* had there not been a Civil Rights movement. I know why I am here. I absolutely know why I am here."

The idea of making up new rules in order to do a superlative job and "endure in the gale force" was a constant theme among all of the Phenomenal women. Emma Chappell was only seventeen years old when she got a job at Continental Bank in Philadelphia. To succeed as a teller, she could have simply modeled herself after the many female employees assigned to low-paying, entry-level positions. To aspire to loftier roles at this time required a vivid imagination, and Emma managed to create a new image for herself. She had no mentors, no role models, and no one willing to show her the ropes. But she had desire.

"When I was coming through, I was made an officer when there were no women officers, black or white. I felt, 'Well, if men can do it, why can't women?' This was before the women's movement. I felt like I could do what the men were doing."

Emma's working experience was unusual in another way—she was destined to spend the next thirty years working at the same bank. "I had about every job in the bank that there was to hold. I worked my way almost to the top of the ladder."

Throughout her climb Emma constantly encountered both racism and sexism. She was never quite sure which one was operating in various incidents. "I think the first time I realized that something was wrong was when I became a loan officer. I couldn't figure out why loans weren't being referred to me, like other people who became officers. They were given a partial portfolio and I wasn't. I was left to create my own.

"I remember going to a loan meeting and being the only black and the only female in the room. When I raised a question, it was belittled. I was made to appear dumb. What was worse, they thought I shouldn't have had the nerve to speak in the first place.

"Initially, I thought it was because I was black. Later, I thought it was really because I was a woman. It went on for years . . . like a silence. You could lose your confidence."

About the same time that Emma became a loan officer, the bank starting hiring black men. "One man they brought in had been involved in sports. They moved him right up. Here I had been all along, working my way up the ladder, and he was zapped up just like that. He was just Mr. Great. Take him right into the board room, then out to the bars, social events, and everything else. I realized that it was not just my color, it was my sex, too."

Crossing the gender line was not easy. "Working relationships are difficult, in that I work in a white man's world and the average white officer of the bank is not going to say, 'Emma, let's go out for a drink.' I don't know if they feel threatened by me, or intimidated or what. That leaves me to find relationships outside of my company. What happens then is they're not actually work relationships, but colleagues in the industry. I'll call up someone I know at another company, just to find out what's happening in my own company."

In their various jobs, sisters always had to be cautious that their attempts to form professional relationships were not misinterpreted as sexual interest. Sexual harassment in high places was a new phenomenon that accompanied progress by women. Black women were particularly vulnerable. Throughout their history in America sexual exploitation was the inevitable consequence of forced and unremunerated labor. In 1991, Anita Hill's predicament proved that high positions did not guarantee protection, either. The only difference was that black women with influence could try to do something about it.

How does one describe the dilemma black women feel in the workplace? "Why am I being disrespected? Because I'm black? Or because I am female? Because I'm incompetent—or because I'm too competent? Or just because . . . ?"

Emma continued to raise questions and challenge the bank for thirty years. Her memories of that struggle remain vivid. "At every level, I have been challenged. All the time. People already in positions were usually trying to get somewhere themselves. Those who were fairly new didn't know who I was. They just assumed, 'Hey, that has to be the weakest link. Let's pounce on that one.' I experienced discrimination at every level. Its presence is everywhere. Not one particular thing, but a number of things. But it made me a stronger person."

Emma refused to "stay in her place." To keep moving forward she explored every avenue. Her search for new knowledge and new experiences was endless. While working full-time at the bank she enrolled at the Berean Business Institute, Temple University, the American Institute of Banking, and the Stonier Graduate School of Banking, a school specializing in preparing chief executive officers and presidents for the banking industry. She learned to be a team player, and came to understand that big careers were not isolated, individualistic adventures. Somehow Emma resisted pressure to "stay in her place" and efforts to force her away from the power table.

Emma credited her family, the church, and the African American sisterhood with supplying the strength she needed to keep going. She also was aware of her debt to others who came before her. Her awareness of the historical past motivated her to get involved in helping others. Not only did she work daily to break down barriers in the banking industry, but she also continued working after hours in the local neighborhood. Matching the career climb with an ongoing commitment to community service was a model that guided many Phenomenal women. By using her banking skills to aid the black empowerment struggle, Emma became well known for her work as a social activist.

However, her community activities may have slowed her advancement at the bank. "I chose my way. Maybe if I'd been a bit more technical, had blinders on, concentrated specifically on my job—which was to make commercial loans—who's to say that I wouldn't have moved up the ladder faster. But I needed to spend time educating my community, helping my people to understand the banking industry—how to handle their money, what to look to the bank for, how not to be intimidated or feel threatened by it, trying to bridge the gap between the big corporate world, the financial world, and the community itself. I probably could have had more influence in the banking industry if I had been more selfish about it. But I've always considered that, in my way, I was doing God's work."

Emma found her place on that historical continuum that continues pushing blacks and women forward. "I have benefited both directly and indirectly from Equal Opportunity, affirmative action, and any and all of those policies to assist black folks. Without them, I wouldn't have been moved ahead. It all has to do with the success of people of color."

Cynthia McKinney's intentions were similar, but her career path was quite different. Instead of working her way up in one institution, she zigzagged her way toward the top. In 1978, Cynthia completed her undergraduate degree in international relations from the University of Southern California. (She is currently a Ph.D. candidate in international relations at Tufts University's Fletcher School of Law and Diplomacy.)

In 1984, when she was twenty-nine years old, Cynthia worked as a Diplomatic Fellow at Spelman College in Atlanta. She also taught political science at Clark Atlanta University and most recently at Agnes Scott College, a women's college in De Kalb County, Georgia. In 1988 Cynthia was elected to the Georgia House of Representatives, where she served alongside her father, Representative Billy McKinney. The general opinion of the legislature was that she would be a nonstarter. Cynthia was dismissed as an ineffective pretty little black woman following in her daddy's footsteps. She quickly showed them what she could do.

She worked on Civil Rights issues, including economic opportunities for minority- and women-owned businesses and environmental justice. Early on, she earned a reputation as a "barn burner." The day after the Persian Gulf war started she made a speech to the Georgia State Legislature condemning the use of force before diplomatic channels had been exhausted. Two-thirds of her colleagues walked out on her. She also protested vigorously against a major landfill being placed in the mostly black Hancock County, which she called an act of "environmental racism."

In the 1990 census, it became clear that Georgia was due a new congressional seat. Of Georgia's ten House delegates, only one was black. Even so, legislative leaders insisted that the state's black communities were so spread out that it would be impossible to draw a new district strong enough to elect another African American to Congress.

McKinney disagreed. "Things are possible," she told the *National Journal*, "if the will is there to do it." During all-night sieges at the computer, she pored over reams of statistics and eventually, with the help of lawyers from the ACLU, cobbled together a new majority black district.

In fact, after all the numbers were thoroughly crunched, she had succeeded in creating *two* new congressional districts, including the Eleventh, which embraced a new grouping of twenty-two counties rambling 250 miles from the Atlanta suburbs down to Savannah, and ending at the seacoast. From the new Eleventh, Cynthia would later launch her own campaign for the United States House of Representatives.

After graduating from Indiana University Law School, Pamela Carter set out to establish herself in a legal career. She immediately found herself severely encumbered by gender and racist discrimination. "I experienced overt racism in courts throughout central and southern Indiana. One court would not formally recognize me as a lawyer. There was a motion, automatically granted, that I would be denied. It was one of those blatant acts, and, of course, we got it overturned. But the point was made."

Other experiences were more insidious, and often Pamela could not be certain whether racism or sexism was taking the leading role. "I was always challenged by white men. Now, I have a lot of oratorical skills, and I had everything on paper that everyone else had. I'm an advocate. Except for my resistance, they would have pushed me over into other areas. When I'd go into court, the other side always looked relieved that I was just a little black woman. I liked that, because then I'd really beat them!"

Sisters who worked their way to the verge of assuming positions of power in the eighties included grassroots activists who had spent years working hard in the trenches battling the status quo, as well as younger, highly trained technocrats. Despite their age differences and their various experiences on the way up, all had to withstand and prevail over the blurring hostilities of racism and sexism.

They coped in two extremely effective ways that have served many determined, highly motivated women: First, no matter what job they were in, they always looked beyond their immediate duties and took on other tasks that needed doing. No job was too hard or too demeaning. They turned in spectacular performances even in the most minimal job.

But doing their jobs well was only part of their equation. Second, they always developed and maintained ties with the African American community and contributed their skills to community service. Their contributions made them even more visible on the local and, eventually, national scene.

The difficulties with antagonists had no clear answers. Black women were aware that they embodied the struggle of both Civil Rights groups and women's rights groups, and they wanted to remain representative of each. The question was, Who could they rely on for support?

One recent attempt to join other women in the political arena provided a modern example of bonding and betrayal. C. Delores Tucker has spent all of her life fighting for black freedom. A longtime activist in the NAACP, she also served as Pennsylvania's secretary of state. As chair for the Democratic National Committee Black Caucus within the national Democratic Party, she was privy to behind-the-scenes political double-dealing.

"I was with Jesse Jackson when he went to see Walter Mondale at the NAACP national convention in Kansas City in 1984. Jesse asked him why he had not interviewed a black woman for vice-president. Mondale said he didn't know any. Jesse gave him six names, and I happened to be one of those he mentioned.

"Later, I served as chair of the Arrangements Committee for Jesse at the Democratic National Convention. That meant going with him to San Francisco to make sure that he had everything that every other candidate had. Even before we got there, Mondale had interviewed black men, white men, and white women as vice-presidential possibilities. He had not interviewed a single black woman.

"Before the convention, black women delegates made an agreement with our white sisters to work the floor together. We agreed to use a whip system, to whip friends into line to support us on affirmative action, on the peace initiative, on voting rights, on no first-right use for miliary weapons of war, and a few other issues that Jesse had on his platform. The white sisters' network was committed to work the floor with us.

"Then they made a deal with Mondale. If he gave them Geraldine Ferraro as vice-president, they would not argue on any of his positions. After Ferraro's nomination, they left us on the issues and we were there on our own. Nobody with us at all.

"Jesse challenged us, 'When are you black women going to speak up for yourselves? Who is going to speak for you? I spoke for you. Now, when are you going to speak for yourselves?'

"We decided then and there that never again would we depend on anybody but ourselves. That we would organize and speak and fight for what we felt were purely the interests and needs of black people. One month later, we came together on Capitol Hill and I presided over the founding of the National Political Congress of Black Women."

Their struggle for respect and fair treatment continued. To a great extent, their ages determined the specific jobs they were in, but whatever their jobs the current group of black women leaders lived through an unprecedented period of social upheaval in which their futures were transformed. They all began to arrive at the power table at the same time. Without fully realizing it, they were getting ready to shape a new model of leadership that drew strength from their social legacy and their creative visions of the future.

7

Leap to the Top

In the last twenty to twenty-five years, African American women have said, 'Ummm, I think it is my time to step up to the plate because ain't nobody else seems to do it quite the way I think it should be done.' We have learned that you can't wait to have somebody else do it. For us, fairy tales don't have quite the same resonance.

When the stuff got down and dirty on the issue of choice, I don't know where we would have been if it hadn't been for a sister like Faye Wattleton stepping up to bat. Always so eloquent, so clear about what she was doing and why she was doing it, so totally unflappable. This is what is going on with black women. We are clear about the life-and-death nature of struggle and what it's done to us. It's going to have to be the African American woman who steps up to the plate. I mean, the whole damn house is on fire!

—*Marcia Gillespie*
Editor in Chief, Ms. *magazine*

Unita Blackwell, mayor of Mayersville, Mississippi, was willing to be interviewed, but she wanted to know exactly how her story would be used. Just as Fannie Lou Hamer was "sick and tired of being sick and tired," Mayor Blackwell was sick and tired of writers, researchers, and newscasters investigating, reporting, and exploiting black folks who were actively involved in the Civil Rights movement. She explained that a "lot of crazy stuff was going on out there."

"I need to check things out," she said. "It's not easy nowadays with a lot of demands from everybody to talk to me. I'm trying to understand who these people are, and why they're always gathering information."

It was at the end of a long day, way past 11 P.M. Unita Blackwell said she was accustomed to being up late because she needed, always, to watch out for the Klan. Only after receiving assurances that what she said would not be misconstrued did she begin to talk freely. Even then, there were moments when she seemed to have second thoughts, but she continued. She was warm, open, and inspiring. Unita had forged a path to leadership seldom imagined by African American women of her generation, and at the age of sixty-one, she remained ready for battle.

Unlimited energy, a constant state of readiness, and a continuous stream of new ideas characterized Phenomenal women as they became nationally recognized and moved into top slots in their various fields. Unita Blackwell provided a sterling example.

Unita first gained prominence as a Civil Rights activist in the early sixties when Mississippi was the most dangerous state in the Union. Often without food on the table or money to pay the rent, Unita and other Mississippi freedom fighters were in the streets and going from door to door registering black folks to vote.

By the seventies the focus of the Civil Rights movement began to shift from voter registration to economic development. Now, with threats on her life continuing, Unita relentlessly began looking for ways to create jobs, develop businesses, and build housing. "We can't separate one piece from another," she said. "If we had not first laid the groundwork with voter registration drives, we couldn't get funding and other support for economic development."

Her move to power was not motivated by personal ambition.

In 1976 Unita engineered her small rural village of Mayersville into an incorporated city because it was the only way she could think of to help her people apply for available federal funding and improve their standard of living. "I am a planner and an organizer. I plan for the people. And I plan to survive."

Once Mayersville was incorporated, Unita became the first black woman mayor in Mississippi. It was an unprecedented leap to power, which brought her immediate national recognition.

Unita immediately used all of her political savvy to apply for city development funding from every possible source. She collected enough money to pave all of Mayersville's dirt streets, install a new water system that reached every home, and a sewage system that reached most. She discovered a way to make her city eligible to receive federal monies to buy land for a new housing development for the elderly and disabled. Building was delayed when the cost of the land rose above the federal limit. Unita reconfigured, renegotiated, reapplied, and somehow persuaded the government to refinance the twenty-unit development, which opened in 1987. On top of that, her creative thinking bought the citizens a new $50,000 fire truck. When you consider that Mayersville's entire projected budget for one year was only $30,000 you get some idea of her achievement. Her own annual salary was a modest $6,000, "If we have it."

Unita's mayoral success attracted attention all around the country. She became involved in the National Conference of Black Mayors, which included the big-city mayors of Newark, Detroit, Los Angeles, Philadelphia, and Washington, D.C. In these conferences she was no small-town bystander. Unita was so respected by the other mayors that the overwhelmingly male organization made her its vice-president.

On July 2, 1992, Unita Blackwell again made national headlines when she was named a MacArthur Fellow, for which she received a $350,000 award. The MacArthur grant is awarded without spending restrictions to "people of genius." The grant recognized and reconfirmed Unita's extraordinary achievement in American society.

"It's just a blessing," Blackwell told a reporter from *Jet* magazine on the day she was informed of the award. Congratulatory calls came in around the clock from people all over the world. Even though she had not yet had time to weigh her options, she said, "I will continue to do the work I've been doing and maybe some other kinds of things, because my mind is freer in terms of wondering about financial strains that I used to go through every month trying to figure out how to pay my bills." Unita wanted people to know, if they never remembered anything else about her, that "I am a person who believed that the impossible sometimes is possible. That I love God. And that I love my people."

Connection to God and devotion to their people were the two most powerful motivators for many of the women participating in this investigation. To see women like Unita Blackwell and Willie Barrow in action is to recognize the legacy that modern black women leaders have inherited from the past. Although the style modulates somewhat from woman to woman, its authenticity is so consistent among them that it must spring from a mutual source. Obviously, being black and female provided a common root. More tantalizing, however, was the striking similarity in which they went about doing business.

Some scholars believe that black women possess an intuitive imprint of their historical past, what poet and author Haki Madhubuti calls a genetic or "epic" memory. Others say that they share a common cultural memory derived from folktales, stories, and images told in our families and passed down. But whatever makes modern black women conduct themselves as warriors in the fight for freedom and dignity, it did not begin in our time.

Phenomenal women believe that the helping and caring traditions of generations of black women are permanently etched in our cultural memories and collective spirit, and from them comes the source of their strength and the fortitude of their convictions.

In truth, contemporary black women leaders can look back to a long and noble line of women, famous in their lifetimes but largely forgotten by history. In David Sweetman's *Women Leaders in African History,* the story begins in 1485 B.C.E. A woman named Hatshepsut became the most powerful individual in ancient Egypt when she seized the throne from her nephew. She immediately surrounded herself with competent advisers and committed herself to developing her nation through agriculture and trade, a concept opposite to the male ruling style, which was obsessed with expanding Egypt's domains through waging war.

At least seven great queens ruled Africa's second great civilization, the great city-state of Meroë, during its golden age. Legend has it that Bartare, the first queen of Meroë, made it her business to create an enlightened society sensitive to the rights of women.

Later, in the sixteenth century, Amina, queen of West Africa, founded the massive Hausa empire, south of the Sahara, which today is known as Nigeria. Unlike Hatshepsut, Amina was a warrior queen, using war to expand and maintain her empire. Her fame as the warrior queen continued to flourish long after her death, and she is still celebrated by those who remember her as a woman who conquered whole nations.

One hundred years later, at the dawn of the African holocaust, came Ann Nzinga, half-sister to Ngola Mbandi, the weak and tyrannical ruler of Angola. When Mbandi ran away from the Portuguese invaders, Nzinga negotiated with the enemy in his place. She outwitted the colonialist governor in treaty making, but when news of the treaty reached the Portuguese government, it immediately canceled the deal. Nzinga stood her ground and formed her people into a guerrilla army, which she personally led. She held her lands without giving an inch for fifty years. Nzinga also surrounded herself with competent advisers and drew on their wisdom. Her rule was marked by tenacity, flexibility, and spirit. The story of the queen who never surrendered became an inspiration to her successors.

In West Africa the Asante people established another great empire, which thrived despite constant battles with the British. Toward the end of the nineteenth century, the empire finally began to disintegrate. Facing almost certain defeat, the people turned to a woman named Yaa Asantewa for leadership. During a visit from the British governor, she launched a surprise attack against the British. Yaa Asantewa fought ceaselessly for three months. In the end, it took more than two thousand British soldiers firing modern weaponry to capture her. She was exiled to an island in the British-held Seychelles northeast of Madagascar, where she lived for another twenty years until her death in 1921.

The hallmarks of these historical women were their bold, unexpected moves and an unshakable belief in the righteousness of their mission. The same characteristics were clearly evident as black women moved onto the world stage in the war against enslavement. The true life stories of Sojourner Truth and Harriet Tubman are legendary in American history, foreshadowing both the modern Civil Rights and women's movements.

Sojourner Truth, born enslaved, was a fiery child of God who would go to any lengths to prove her point and rally others to her cause. Along with Mary Ann Shadd Cary she was the first to link the fight for racial freedom with women's rights. Truth would never dilute the fight for black women's rights in order to concentrate attention on slavery. Today, her name still symbolizes the dual struggle that black women face between race and gender.

Harriet Tubman was also born to enslaved parents who managed to provide their children with a strong, nurturing family life, steeped in Christian religion and African folklore. She also believed she was on a mission from God, a belief that sustains many modern black women leaders as well. Harriet Tubman worked with everyone—men, women, blacks, whites, people of all religions—willing to help in the battle to free her people. Tubman was small in stature, but bold in deeds and daring. Trekking dangerous back roads in the South she sang out loudly in the night, calling forward from their hiding places terrorized black men and women. More than one hundred years after her death, she is still called the Moses of her people.

Ida B. Wells-Barnett, Anna Julia Cooper, Josephine St. Pierre Ruffin, Mary Church Terrell, and Mary McLeod Bethune—their names and deeds ring out. Many of the women interviewed for this book said their personal role model growing up had been Mary McLeod Bethune, one of the most influential black women of the twentieth century.

Bethune was born ten years after the Emancipation Proclamation, one of seventeen children growing up in a strongly religious household in South Carolina. All her life she heard about the atrocities of slavery from her parents and some of her older siblings. Bethune's heart's desire was to bring education and the Christian faith to Africa. She studied at the Bible Institute for Home and Foreign Missions, but after graduation was rejected for missionary service in Africa because she was black.

The irony of the rejection was not lost on her. Deeply disappointed, she cast about for another role in which to make her contribution. As is often the case with strong personalities, rejection fueled ambition. "With five little girls, a buck and a half, and a belief in God," Bethune founded the Daytona Educational and Industrial Institute in Daytona, Florida, in 1904. The little school's survival was tenuous, but Bethune hung on and passionately went about promoting education for black girls in the community. Eventually, financial help came from the black church, socially prominent white women, and white male philanthropists like James N. Gamble of Proctor & Gamble. Today, Bethune-Cookman College is a four-year, fully accredited liberal arts college that enrolls more than 2,100 full-time students. Bethune's impassioned belief in education as the key to racial uplift left an indelible stamp on the modern Civil Rights movement.

She didn't stop there. Her visionary agenda demanded that black women would never again be shut out of shaping the nation's social agenda. She founded the National Council of Negro Women, which became the first all-black group to operate in the nation's capital.

Black clubwomen broke the ground for the future by organizing and setting platforms and directions. Among many others, past and present, Dr. Dorothy Height has been president of the National Council of Negro Women for the past thirty-nine years; Dr.

LaFrances Rodger-Rose is founder and president of the International Congress of Black Women; Dr. Bertha Maxwell Roddey is president of Delta Sigma Theta; Jewell Jackson McCabe is chairwoman of the National Coalition of 100 Black Women; and Dr. Wynetta Frazier is president of National Hook-Up of Black Women Inc.

Through her own development of all-black women's groups, Mary McLeod Bethune became the first American black woman ever to walk the corridors of national power. In 1939 she was appointed as the director of the Division of Negro Affairs of the National Youth Administration, making her the highest-ranking black woman in government, and a member of Franklin Roosevelt's "unofficial black cabinet."

Her position with the Roosevelt administration, particularly her personal relationship with Eleanor Roosevelt, gave her tremendous influence on national policies. Bethune was suddenly catapulted to national prominence, creating an important role for black women where no role had ever before existed. Watching her every move, the American public was forced to admit that it was at least possible for a black woman to lead and to speak fairly for all.

Down each new path, McLeod challenged racism and sexism, and never flagged. Every black schoolchild in America knew her name and knew what she stood for. While some disagreed with her self-deprecating tactics, she was the most exceptional black woman of her time.

When she died in May of 1955, the nation was verging on a social movement that would permanently alter race relations in this country. Within a few years, sister activists like Fannie Lou Hamer, Angela Davis, and Shirley Chisholm stormed the front pages and added renewed strength and youthful boldness to black female leadership style.

Fannie Lou Hamer, the uneducated child of a Mississippi sharecropper, threw herself into grassroots activism and channeled her fighting spirit into organizations that promised to improve conditions for her struggling, impoverished community. She was driven by her deep religious conviction and intense rage over racial injustice.

She fought wherever the battle took her, and never gave up an inch of integrity. Hamer became vice-chairperson of the Mississippi Freedom Democratic Party, which was challenging the segregated Democratic Party of the South. Her defining moment came in 1964 in a speech from the floor of the Democratic National Convention in Atlantic City. "I'm so sick and tired of being sick and tired," she said, with frustration aching in her voice. The soul of the nation was stirred.

Shirley Chisholm made history in 1968 when she became the first black woman elected to Congress. In 1972 she did it again when she became the first black person, man or woman, to seek the Democratic nomination for president. Throughout the seventies Chisholm personified the cutting edge of leadership, challenging both male- and white-dominated politics. Her bold, dedicated style bore the fresh imprint of her immediate predecessors and owed an even larger debt to her long-ago ancestors. The idea of spirit women from the past influencing their modern-day sisters evoked the African spiritual concept called *Sankofa*—looking back in order to move forward.

On July 22, 1993, Senator Carol Moseley-Braun grasped the ancestral arc with an impassioned oratory that stopped Jesse Helms in his tracks. Senator Helms was trying to help the United Daughters of the Confederacy renew the patent on their organization's emblem, which featured the Confederate flag. Helms and Senator Strom Thurmond had sneaked in language to that effect as an amendment to the National Service Bill. As a larger, surefire bill wins Senate approval, such "tagalong" amendments are often swept along unnoticed. But the freshman senator from Illinois *had* noticed. She tried to bury the measure in the Judiciary Committee. When that didn't work, she resorted to high drama. On a first pass, the Senate voted fifty-two to forty-eight in favor of the amendment.

An outraged Moseley-Braun seized the Senate floor. "On this issue there can be no consensus," she admonished. "It is an outrage. It is an insult. It is absolutely unacceptable to me and to millions of Americans, black or white, that we would put the imprimatur of the

United States Senate on a symbol of this kind of idea. This flag is the real flag of the Confederacy."

The flag, she said, was a symbol of slavery, and represented a bloody war that had been "fought to keep the states from separating themselves over the issue of whether or not my ancestors could be held as property, as chattel, as objects of trade and commerce in this country. This is no small matter."

Using the time-honored threat of the filibuster, she held the floor while Senate leaders scurried to arrange a second vote. As word of her fervent oration spread through Senate offices, other senators rose and asked to speak. One after another, they took the floor to praise her, until even Senator Howell Heflin of Alabama, whose family, he said, was "rooted in the Confederacy," reversed his vote. On the second round, twenty-seven senators changed their votes to stand with Moseley-Braun, and the amendment failed, seventy-five to twenty-five.

It was more than the righteousness of her position that won over her colleagues. Senator Ted Kennedy said that Moseley-Braun had given them reason to believe again in their own purpose. "Although the Senate calls itself the world's greatest deliberative body," Kennedy said, "we don't listen to each other. We have our minds made up before we vote and simply wait our turn to get up and talk. That's what makes this moment historic. I'm very grateful to her for reminding us what we're here for."

Impassioned, brilliant, as if she had been rehearsing this speech all of her life—as in one way or another she had—on this particular day, Senator Moseley-Braun embodied the promise of her ancestors.

Throughout history black women have led from the fields and from the mountains; they have organized their troops while sitting at kitchen tables and in church pews; they have protested in front of convention centers and at the back of buses, at rallies in the streets of Chicago, and with speeches from the floor of the House of Representatives. They have left an indelible image in the memories of their descendants: fiery spirit, religious devotion, and an uncompromising belief in their ability to achieve the impossible.

Late one night Willie Barrow was giving a reporter from *Time* magazine a big piece of her mind. While he was trying to investigate the finances of PUSH, dozens of other media people were trying to get a story to explain and exploit the Chicago teachers' strike in 1987, the longest ever in that city, which has the nation's third-largest school system. The governor, state legislature, school board, teachers' union, and the parents of Chicago's 432,000 students were all involved.

Unlike many celebrated cases in the past in which the African American community was pitted against white administrators and union officials, Chicago's black folks were fighting among themselves.

Some school board members, some representatives of the teachers' union, and 60 percent of the students and parents were black. Even Harold Washington, the mayor of Chicago, was black. On the surface, then, the conflict raging among the various parties didn't inherently appear to be caused by racism alone. But if race was taken off the table, what were the real issues? A conflict over teaching methods? An ideological battle over the purpose and goals of education? Or, God forbid, a class struggle between upper-, middle-, and lower-class black folks?

Requests from beleaguered community leaders and parents' groups poured into PUSH headquarters, located in the heart of Chicago's black community, asking Reverend Barrow to help refocus the issues and bring the strike to an end.

The main stumbling block to a settlement was the demand by teachers that they receive an 8.5 percent raise in the first year of a new contract, and about 5 percent in the second year. The board of education was proposing to *cut* teachers' salaries.

On Friday night, forty-five days into the strike, the room was packed with worried parents and community leaders unloading scathing criticism onto the teachers' union. Reverend Barrow rose to speak, her deceptively diminutive presence silencing the audience.

She asked both sides to rethink their priorities and focus on the best interests of the children. Some folks, she said, had become "so high and mighty they have forgotten where they come from."

Gently, she reminded everyone of who they were as a people: Black folks with a long history of struggle. Amid parents' angry accusations that the teachers were greedy and selfish, she managed to calm the storm. "Together we can work this out." The sister was powerful and she knew it.

Immediately following the meeting, parents, community leaders, and teachers held a press conference to announce that they were unified in a collective effort to bring an end to the strike, and within days the seemingly intractable situation was resolved.

Willie Barrow had taken over the leadership of PUSH directly from the hands of Jesse Jackson. This is how she described her transition to power: "When Reverend Jackson decided to run in 1983, everybody thought he would never leave PUSH in order to campaign. When he left, I left with him because he said, 'I can't run unless Willie goes with me.' He got somebody to carry on here while we ran.

"I was his deputy road manager, and coordinated all across the nation and Cuba and Nicaragua—the whole thing, all around the world. When he did not win, he developed the Rainbow Coalition, and he sent me back to put PUSH back together.

"Everybody was waiting still for him to come back. Intellectually, they knew he was gone, but emotionally they couldn't deal with it. So when I took it over, they had a hard time adjusting. We carry a lot of volunteers, about three or four hundred. They couldn't deal with Reverend Jackson not being here, so they sort of sat on the sidelines and waited—'Let's see what she's going to do.' A few of the volunteers left, but none of the staff left.

"After that, the organization started building like a whirlwind. I mean, we have never met with as many ministers monthly as we meet with now. I meet with 150 ministers each month. I always say to them, 'I feel that I am supported, guided, bound, and backed up when all of you great ministers are here.' And we have women ministers now. Out of 150, we have at least 25 or 30 women."

Unita Blackwell's and Willie Barrow's sense of direction and purpose were always clear to them. However, younger women, with many more choices open to them, often had trouble knowing which road to take. Such was the case with Marcia Gillespie.

After ten years, *Essence* magazine was an unqualified success, and it was time for Marcia to move on, although she did not know where. Leaving the country was a viable option. Marcia moved to Jamaica. "I wanted to have the experience of living in a black environment. It was the best thing I ever did. I lived there on and off for three years. It is my second home.

"I did very little at first. Then I started doing some writing and ended up teaching at the University of the West Indies. It was really about me taking a moment. I had been on such a fast track, it really was about me refinding myself. A period of reflection."

Eventually, she knew it was time to get into the swing of things when a young sister approached her and said, "Didn't you use to be somebody famous?" Marcia said, "I cherish the moment."

Marcia had served as executive editor of *Ms.* magazine in the late eighties and also wrote a column for the magazine. In 1991 *Ms.* charted a bold new course, becoming the first popular magazine in history to refuse advertising. Gloria Steinem's editorial proclaimed: "We intend to speak our truths, unfettered, unhindered." After steering the magazine through this change, Steinem, the magazine's original editor in chief, then passed the reins of leadership to Robin Morgan.

"Robin asked me if I wanted to stay," Marcia said. "And I said, 'No, I don't think you can afford me, girlfriend.' At the time, Robin was doing a project for the UN, and she said, 'Would you be interested in doing this?' I said, 'Sure, great.' We have that kind of relationship. Robin took over *Ms.* and I went to the UN." Marcia also started consulting for the *New York Times*.

One day, she received a casual phone call from Robin. "I didn't know what she was calling about. We said we would have lunch. When she asked me about taking over *Ms.*, I was floored. She was real clear that she had only wanted to run the magazine for three years, maximum. She wanted to go back to writing. And she was real clear, too, that she wanted to turn it over to a woman of color.

"I was very surprised. I never expected to be an editor in chief again, unless it was for another black publication. I couldn't say 'yes' right away."

Marcia had two major questions to contemplate. "I know how demanding running a magazine is. I love it, but I wasn't sure I wanted to do it again in an even more stress-filled situation. And I wasn't sure I wanted to take on feminist politics." *Ms.* symbolized the women's movement which was, in the opinion of many, comprised of white, middle-class, bra-burning, male-bashing, left-wing, lesbian-loving, radical feminists. The movement had repeatedly failed to attract black women in large numbers.

After pondering her decision, Marcia recognized that the job was a window of opportunity for black women. "It's very important that we try to open doors. I asked myself, 'Can you be of service?' I realized, 'Absolutely, yes!' "

Marcia's Gillespie's appointment in 1993 as editor in chief of *Ms.* magazine was a benchmark achievement for black women and a stunning victory for all sisters, black and white. She was the first black woman in history to head a mainstream women's magazine, one of the most highly competitive, pressure-filled slots in the publishing industry.

Her appointment opened up new avenues for black women, affirming that women of color could take the lead. It also meant that an entire generation of black women, already hooked on Marcia's wisdom, could further examine women's issues and ask, "What is this feminist thing all about?" Marcia hoped to develop a magazine with a new agenda where all women would be part of the discussion.

Marcia arrived at *Ms.* a seasoned sister: professional, credentialed, and, most importantly, honed in the struggle. She knew where she stood on the issues: Marcia would not waver on her commitment to civil rights, human rights, black men, and black women. She was equally committed to the vision of African American women and other women of color "engaging in the discussion and the dynamic of what the women's movement and feminism ought to be." Marcia is determined to make *Ms.* into a magazine as diverse and inclusive as the women's movement ought to be.

Phenomenal women moving into top slots often found the transition a rough one. All of the women had experienced both support and hostility throughout their careers. When they reached for the top, they found they were often bitterly resented, sometimes by their own sisters and brothers. They needed to toughen their skins and put on their armor to survive. The transition was made more harrowing when the hostility came from unexpected places.

In 1991, Pamela Carter, the little Indiana girl who let her friend win the track race so his father wouldn't humiliate him, decided to run for public office. Pamela received tremendous support from black women, who viewed her move up the political ladder as a giant leap forward. White women also supported her. However, she was disappointed not to receive the full support of black men.

"There had always been subtle challenges, but when I ran for office it was blatant. I was out there on my own. In fairness, in the early stages I was running against a black man. Many people thought the party should have backed him, but it backed me instead. So they had a legitimate focus for their discontent. Later on, it went well beyond that. They knew it and I knew it. Did they vote for me? Yes, probably. Did they send some contributions? Yes, probably. But it was halfhearted at best. They really didn't think I should win or could win. I was surprised that it would be that blatant."

The worst battering, however, came from her white male opponent. In a bruising campaign, Timothy Bookwalter carted around a life-size cardboard cutout of Carter so the public could "see" her.

"Some people asked me if I would put my picture on my own signs. Of course I would. I wouldn't want anyone to vote for me if they didn't know I was a black female. People often run away from that, because they think if you're black you can't be a variety of other things as well. But you have to start with being proud of who you are."

Pamela credited her parents with giving her the strength and security that became her personal trademarks. "My parents were proud of their race. They didn't distinguish between people. They were never classist or racist. They were comfortable with who they were and demanded that we be that way as well. They would tell us, 'People who would diminish you in those kinds of ways are not your friends.' I think that helped me a lot."

In 1992 Pamela Carter, who had integrated a CYO camp when she was eight years old, made history when she became the first black and the first woman to be elected attorney general for the state of Indiana. No one in any other state in the union had ever achieved this goal.

The nastiness of the campaign had prepared Pamela for anything, but the final results at the polls were a pleasant surprise:

"I was greeted with enthusiasm in all ninety-two counties. It was much more than people really expected. A confluence of events came together at the right time." More than enough people had supported Pamela to give her a fifty-two-to-forty-eight margin, which meant that she pulled voters from several economic strata and every ethnic and racial group.

"All people wanted was an elected official who listened to them, who cared, and who could adequately represent their interests. They were intrigued by the way I talked. They would mention that a lot, my ability to use English in the same way that they did. They were willing to take a chance."

She is aware that her achievement as a "first" black and "first" woman was more than a matter of personal excellence. She admitted that race and sex may have worked to her advantage in the campaign. "There were a number of agendas in the election, and undoubtedly tokenism was one of them. I recognize that. But there were also broader and more beneficent reasons for me being chosen."

Undoubtedly Pamela Carter intends to represent and serve all of the people of Indiana. At the same time, she carried her strong sense of identity into office with her. "I see myself as first and foremost an African American, and I'm not ashamed of that. African Americans confront a complex social and economic reality. We learn that we have to be there for our folks and I think it would be immoral not to."

On taking office Pamela immediately hired new lawyers and other personnel to staff the attorney general's office. "When I came in there were some blacks on the paralegal and support staff, but no black individuals on the law staff. I decided to clean house. No question about it. I brought in women, and African Americans, and Hispanics, and people with disabilities, the whole range. Our office now looks like what this country and this state look like. These are qualified and capable people who can represent the people of this state as well as anyone, and they have demonstrated that fully. Our office has accumulated more awards in two years than it had in the past twenty-five years."

Not everyone agreed on the desirability of diversity. Older white males who had been part of the previous regime filed suit, claiming they were victims of both race and age discrimination.

"I'm actually being sued for racial discrimination," Pamela said. "It is the utmost irony that people would complain on the diversity in my office. When the status quo is maintained, they never focus on discrimination. That's amazing to me."

Diversity in the workplace is one of the obvious payoffs to black women moving into leadership positions. The offices of other Phenomenal women are also different from those of most other power brokers. The same diversity is present in the congressional offices of Barbara-Rose Collins (D-Mich.), Eva M. Clayton (D-N.C.), Eddie Bernice Johnson (D-Tex.), Carrie P. Meek (D-Fla.), and other political leaders. It is present at Dorothy Brunson's multimillion-dollar communications network and at the headquarters of the National Education Association.

As a result of Pamela Carter's policies, the people of the state of Indiana now find the attorney general's office responsive to its needs, which is Carter's primary goal.

Wherever and whenever they served, the closer they got to taking power, the greater the resistance against them. When asked if people challenged her position, Dr. Deborah Prothrow-Stith, commissioner of public health for the state of Massachusetts, answered with a resounding "Oh, yes!" and went on to give this colorful analogy: "Sometimes it's done in malicious ways. Most of the time, it's by default. People may not throw a harpoon at your heart, but they'll nibble at your ankles until you bleed to death."

Shirley Franklin said that she, too, "got it from everyone." When Mayor Andrew Young first appointed her as Atlanta's chief managing director in 1982, many people thought a female sociologist with primarily academic and art program experience could never make it in the rough and tumble political scene. The response from the brothers ran the gamut—supportive, paternalistic, resistant, hostile. "At first, every black man that I worked with suggested that I was in over my head, that I shouldn't be in the position, and I should delegate my authority to them or someone else. White businessmen and black businessmen were reluctant to talk to me. They didn't think I would be interested in talking about business. Or they thought I didn't know how the game was played.

"I remember a prominent black businessman invited me to a meeting with some other black businesspeople. When he introduced me, he said, 'I've invited Shirley because Andy appointed her to this important position. I don't know why she is not staying home with her children.' He thought that was a warm introduction. He was being paternalistic, looking out for me.

"All of the commissioners were reluctant, some more than others. The ones who expected to get along with me least—because they thought I would make all my decisions based on politics or what was best for Andrew Young—are probably the ones that I got along with best, because my personality is totally unlike that. I always know a whole lot about an issue before I get to a decision-making conclusion.

"One female commissioner resented the fact that I didn't have her style. She felt I was too interested in political ramifications. I don't mean party politics. It's just that some things make more sense for a city that is 60 to 70 percent black and 30 percent poor. I consider that a political issue. She had some resentment."

Other challenges came from political friends and supporters of Mayor Young. "There were frequent charges that 'Andrew Young is fine, it's just all the people around him.' Now, I'm not stupid enough to exclude myself from 'all the people around him.' I think to a large extent that is because I am a black female. I couldn't stand the job if I thought I was incompetent, and I never had any indication from Andy that he thinks it's true. So I just let that roll off my back.

"The truth is, the black community here doesn't really care whether I'm male or female. They expect a black mayor and a black administration to deliver in a particular way. If a woman can do it, fine; if a man can do it, fine. Some think that a man would be forceful, or forceful in a different way. I don't really throw my weight around.

"One day, after about two years, Andy said to me, 'I wanted you to succeed, but I wasn't sure that it wouldn't get too rough and you wouldn't opt out.' I had never felt he didn't have complete confidence in me, even though we disagree a lot of the time. He had gone way out on a limb to appoint me, and it turned out even he had his doubts."

Being the head of one of the nation's most powerful unions is bound to inflate one's ego. However, Mary Hatwood Futrell, when interviewed in her office when she was president of the National Education Association, exuded confidence without arrogance, and strength without aggression. Her office lay in the massive building of the National Education Association (NEA), located in Washington, D.C., in the heart of the policy-making educational district, and emanated power. Futrell presided over her suite of offices and her dedicated staff with a quietly elegant presence. One would never guess how hard her climb has been.

Before she earned the top spot she had spent many years combining community service with her education, teaching career, and administrative jobs. "I remember when the buses were first desegregated, and how afraid people were when they got on to sit in certain areas. But they did it. I remember marching on Petersburg, Virginia, to try to get them to desegregate the stores, the restaurants, the public facilities."

She began working her way up through the NEA, serving in numerous capacities locally, regionally, and ultimately in the national organization. "Each time I ran for office, I ran a full-fledged campaign, so I could earn the right to run again. When I was running for secretary-treasurer of the national NEA, I remember being told that I should not get elected because all I would concentrate on would be issues for minorities. Then they said, 'We shouldn't elect her because she'll get pregnant.' Then it was, 'You can't perform the job because you're a female,' and 'You can't carry all the books around.' " Mary ran and won.

The usual pattern at the NEA is for the president to serve one term, then the vice-president runs for the top slot. In 1983 the vice president decided not to run. Mary, then secretary-treasurer, expected to go back home and resume her teaching career. But several people in NEA asked her to run, a rare event from her position. She won again, although she was by no means universally accepted by the membership.

"The first year, I received hate mail saying that a black woman should not lead the NEA. Now, about half of the NEA presidents had been women, and I was the fourth minority. I was the second black female president. Elizabeth D. Koontz from North Carolina was the first, in 1967. These incidents were very painful, but each one made me grow a little more determined to try to correct racism."

She certainly did overcome. Before Mary Hatwood Futrell's administration, the NEA had revolving-door presidents. Every year a new president was elected, and most did not work full-time. Day-to-day operations were run by staff members. Mary set new, higher standards for the organization. Under her leadership all officials work full-time and elections are held every two years, encouraging everyone to become more committed to his or her responsibilities. The budget has grown to $100 million a year, with 1,860,000 members. Futrell has served an unprecedented three terms (six years) as NEA president.

The themes of service, dedication, and an ability to succeed despite all attempts to turn them back or bring them down were constant among all the women. After thirty years at Continental Bank, one of the largest banking institutions in the city of Philadelphia, Emma Chappell had come a long way. While she had struggled with racism and sexism, overall Emma still felt that Continental Bank had treated her well. She had an impressive title and was making good money. At times, the bank allowed her to do almost anything she wanted to do to build relationships in the black community. Her high visibility made her one of the black community's most credible spokespersons. She frequently said, "I just want to see black people have control over their own economic destiny."

Emma's vision of her responsibility to give back continued to expand. She served as cochair for the successful mayoral campaign for Wilson Goode, Philadelphia's first black mayor. She also served as the national treasurer for the Reverend Jesse Jackson's presidential campaign and organized support for former Congressman William Gray's reelection campaigns. She is a lifetime member of the NAACP.

Emma did not limit her contributions to the African American community. She also served in an executive capacity for the Girl Scouts of the U.S.A., the United Cerebral Palsy Association, and the Forum for Executive Women.

"I feel that I have tremendous influence. I can pick up the phone and make things happen. I am able to mobilize people and mobilize money. If you're able to mobilize for meaningful things, then you are influential. I try to use my influence for good work."

Even as she expanded her work in the community, she never disappointed the bank. When Continental merged with Mid-Atlantic Bank of New Jersey, Emma received a new title: Vice president of the Urban Economic Development Services Department. It sounded terrific, until she learned that she would still report to another senior vice-president, a white male with the same experience and competence as her own.

Despite her dedication, it was clear that the road to the top was blocked. Emma realized that she did not have quite enough power to make real and permanent changes in the banking industry. Without those changes she would never be able to significantly advance black community development.

Languishing in the role of vice-president is an experience shared by many sisters. While their potential is unlimited, many have experienced what they call the "glass ceiling and cement boots" phenomenon.

By all accounts, Joyce Roche, currently executive vice-president of global marketing for Carson Products Company, is one of the most powerful black women in corporate America. Her rise has been documented in both the black press and mainstream media. Joyce was born in 1947 in Iberville, a rural community outside of New Orleans, Louisiana. She and her ten siblings were raised by her mother, with additional support from her aunt, who had nine children of her own. Her family tried to protect her from the harsher aspects of racial discrimination, but growing up in the South "you always knew that you were a Negro."

Joyce attended Dillard University where she received her B.A. degree in math education, then moved on to Columbia for her M.B.A. After a brief stint with City University of New York (CUNY), she joined Avon Products Company. Joyce says that she was lucky to be in the right place at the right time and credits her successful climb to a combination of hard work and the equal opportunity programs that flourished during the seventies: "There's no possible way I could have gained all that I did without affirmative action and other social programs. Without blinking or thinking, I know that without a doubt I have benefited from these efforts." Her career blossomed at Avon. She left the company to join Revlon Products, but returned two years later, eventually landing an executive position as vice-president of gifts and decoratives. This was the first time that she felt she was in a position of power. However, power is an elusive concept. "There's always somebody who has more power than you. I always had to report to someone else, and even the president had to report to the CEO."

Avon was "a really good company to work for," and Joyce remained there for seventeen years, holding virtually every senior executive marketing position. She had a great title—vice-president of global marketing—and excellent pay, but little room for further growth and few opportunities to use the myriad skills that she had acquired over the years. While she dreamed of greater opportunity to reach new goals, she never thought about becoming the president or CEO. "It wasn't within the realm of reality. Avon had only recently appointed their first female president, in 1993, a white woman, and I saw no real possibilities for black women to achieve the same in my lifetime." Realizing that growth opportunities would be limited, she terminated her employment with Avon, took some time to reflect on her future, and then made a lateral move to Carson Products, a smaller company, which she hopes will open up new achievement potential.

Faced with a similar glass ceiling, Emma Chappell made an even riskier choice. In 1991, Emma decided to leave the security of Continental Bank to launch the United Bank of Philadelphia, the first chartered black-owned, full-service commercial bank since 1923. She specifically targeted her bank toward addressing the underserved banking needs of the black community.

The move looked sudden, but Emma had been working on this bold initiative for five years. With the support of black ministers preaching the gospel of economic self-worth, she began to raise the start-up money, eventually coming up with $6 million. Such an investment of trust from the people required her to maintain maximum commitment to the task with a minimum amount of personal ego. With the basic operational belief that no one is an island, Emma surrounded herself with competent, committed people who helped her launch her vision.

Emma's efforts to provide financial services, including personal loans, business loans, and mortgages, to the black community is unprecedented in contemporary America. At a time when the banking industry continued to be plagued by reports of discrimination in lending and service practices, United Bank of Philadelphia was a national model worthy of emulation.

As usual, Emma did a lot more than make loans. The new bank invited neighborhood groups in for special programs on investments and financial planning. High school kids came to learn how to plan and start their own businesses. Resistance from the rest of the banking industry continued to be formidable, and Emma continued to look to the future.

After only two years she once again walked on the national cutting edge of banking when she pulled off a stunning deal that is expected to boost the chances for success of minority-owned banks across America. United was among the first to take advantage of a new law allowing the federal government to turn over failed S and Ls to minority-owned banks. Before the law even passed, Emma had already targeted four white-owned thrifts in minority neighborhoods. She made her move the moment the law was signed. With a few strokes of the pen, Emma transformed United Bank of Philadelphia from a struggling one-office enterprise to a thriving institution with five branches, $100 million in deposits, and a lucrative portfolio of loans.

National recognition came instantly, and requests poured in from minority-owned banks around the country, asking how she did it. "I'm blessed," she told one of the many reporters covering the story. "And the bank is blessed."

Emma's move to the top lit up another common success strategy shared by Phenomenal women: Thorough preparation, followed by swift action. The pattern appeared to be universal among them.

When *Working Woman* magazine set out to find the country's

most admired women managers of 1993, they focused on multitalented candidates who delivered top-quality products or services, achieved great bottom-line results, and who also treated their employees well and also worked to enhance their communities. The magazine's handpicked national panel, comprised of twelve distinguished experts, could come up with only forty candidates in the whole country who fit the description. Ten made the final cut. Gwendolyn Calvert Baker was among them.

Gwendolyn was a former schoolteacher, college professor, and past president of the New York City Board of Education. As a professor, Gwendolyn had gained recognition as a multiculturalist. She studied and wrote about innovative approaches of incorporating different values, lifestyles, and cultural nuances into the education system so that young people would have a greater understanding and appreciation of the world around them, and so that students on the fringes could derive greater benefit from the educational system. Gwendolyn was committed to civil rights and social justice. To put her concepts to work she knew she had to move out of researching and writing and make her way into a top decision-making position. Her plan was to work toward becoming a college president.

But Gwendolyn's plan took a sudden detour. A national headhunter assigned to locate a professional educator with good credentials and moral commitment found Gwendolyn's name and called her. Gwendolyn's interest was piqued when the agent told her that a national organization wanted to eliminate racism.

The spirit of all the ancestors began to work its magic. "I'll never forget when I said, 'Let me talk to you about this.' We made an appointment and I met her down at the Hyatt. When she told me it was the YWCA of the USA, I almost had a heart attack.

"When I was a teenager back in Ann Arbor, Michigan, I was a Y Teen. But I couldn't actually go into the YWCA because blacks weren't allowed. I had to participate through the community center, which is where all of my extracurricular activity was housed."

Gwendolyn knew she had received a sign. No sooner had she accepted the challenge, however, when she discovered that, as is often the case, a black woman had been brought on board after the ship was sinking. The YWCA was swamped with a half-million-dollar budget deficit. The staff at the national headquarters in New York often had to wait months for the board to meet before they could act on anything. Morale was at an all-time low. The YWCA's image as a powerful advocate for women had faded away to nothing.

Gwendolyn's immediate tactic was to show the board she could refloat the ship in a hurry. She began by redesigning and renegotiating the cumbersome, seventy-thousand-square-foot office space of the national headquarters, a maneuver projected to save $12 million over the next seventeen years. After that impressive introduction, the board gave her the freedom to cut other costs, computerize operations, and revitalize the organization's role as a social innovator.

It was a good start, but it wasn't enough. Operating costs continued to climb and contributions continued to slide during the national recession. Gwendolyn intensified her efforts. She surveyed individual member associations to find out what they needed and expected from headquarters. At every level of analysis and planning, she kept the board and affiliates informed and involved.

Information pouring in from the member associations convinced Gwendolyn to focus sharply on renewing the YWCA's advocacy role for women and people of color. Once she had the data to support her, she moved fast. She immediately implemented a policy of working with nonprofit foundations to develop programs to combat racism and sexual harassment. She created a stronger research division to help member organizations design better community programs, which she called Project Redesign.

Gwendolyn implemented her changes in just seven months. The result was phenomenal. By reducing the national office staff by half—a painful process that she eased by offering early-retirement packages and outplacement services to employees whose jobs were eliminated—Gwendolyn cut annual expenses by a whopping 45 percent. Meanwhile, the research division's findings sparked a partnership with the Centers for Disease Control and Prevention and Avon

Products to set up and maintain breast-cancer support and prevention programs in all of the country's YWCA member associations.

When interviewed in 1987 Gwendolyn was in top form. "I have never felt better," she said. "I would just wish that I had more time to do more things." Apparently she found it.

In 1994 Gwendolyn was named president of the U.S. Committee for UNICEF, the oldest and largest of thirty-five national committees that comprise the United Nations Children's Fund. Her new appointment brought a staff of 125 and an annual budget of $50 million. Her top priorities include educating American children about children living in other parts of the world, and increasing the volunteer pool and donations. UNICEF serves children worldwide, and Gwendolyn is aware that her committee is strategically positioned to benefit the lives of African American children.

"If we can begin to pull our children away from just thinking about their plight," she told *Essence* magazine, "if we can begin to expose them to the way things are done in other places, we will begin to build a stronger group of African American children who will be much more world oriented."

All of their stories about life at the top made clear that race and gender issues do not disappear when a woman becomes powerful and successful. Pamela Carter offered this cautionary warning to those who attempt to follow in their footsteps: "Black women should always know that they will have to continue to fight. If you win an office, the next day you're starting all over again. You have to demand and earn respect from your staff. There was a great deal of excitement when I won the attorney general's office. It was an historic achievement. I had momentum coming in. But you still have to earn respect every day. In very latent ways, gender and race bias are here. Class bias is here, too. Did you go to the right schools? It's surmountable, but it's a reality, and you have to work to overcome it."

Even though all the women were aware of this fundamental reality, two still suffered major setbacks after they reached the top.

Thirty-eight-year-old Cynthia McKinney is a youngster among the nation's powerful black women, but she embodies the same strength and vision of her older sisters. Like many Phenomenal women she acquired the notion of public service in the bosom of her parents, who were activists in the Civil Rights movement. She drew particular support from her father, who had gained political savvy through his work as a Georgia state legislator. "There's not much my dad hasn't seen, in terms of the Machiavellian maneuvering, posturing, and backstabbing that happens in politics. You have to be aware of positioning three moves down the road. I always rely on his good counsel."

When Cynthia entered the five-candidate Democratic primary for Georgia's new Eleventh Congressional District in the summer of 1992, the old boys in the Georgia State Legislature said she'd be lucky to finish fifth.

"The reason I got into the race was because we had to fight so hard to create this district. I was the scorn of every editorial page in Georgia for fighting for the congressional plans that we have now. Then when I saw the prospective candidates who were being talked around in the press by the political pundits, it was the same old stuff. We couldn't just give the district away to somebody who's not going to do anything. To see all my work going to benefit politicians who didn't care one bit about the people I was fighting for, well. . . .

"Down in Georgia the way you move up the political ladder, the way you got your chairmanship, the way you got on a committee, or a special title behind your name was because, whatever you were after, you were willing to compromise to get it. Now, what was it you were willing to compromise? You were willing to compromise on your blackness.

"Those who compromised on their blackness, those who compromised on the black agenda, those who never acknowledged that there might even be a black agenda—they were the ones the white leadership pointed to and said, 'This is our person who can represent us in a very special way. This is our black man, this is our black person, this is our black girl.'

"When we looked at those candidates, we saw people who each step of the way, as they ascended that ladder of success, left a little piece of themselves behind. They certainly left their black constituents who voted them into office behind. So I offered myself as a candidate. The people understood why."

When she entered the race Cynthia wrote to all of the women in Congress. Maxine Waters was the first to respond. "She sent me my first money. Even her husband took me on when I was campaigning. I used to call his office; he didn't know me from Adam, but I used to explain all the problems I was having and he would sit there and listen.

"In the primary we didn't have any big names supporting us. We didn't have the economic elite. One candidate had the governor out campaigning for him, hopscotching and helicoptering, living large, and doing all the things that money can bring to a campaign. The other candidate had the speaker of the Georgia State Legislature for him. You would have thought the speaker would have campaigned for me, just to get rid of the big thorn in his side. These were two black males, and on primary election night they were the ones being profiled on television as being the contenders. No media even came to my victory party because I was not expected to win.

"My candidacy represented an opportunity for ordinary people to reject that notion of political promotion and, instead, to promote somebody whose whole reason for being in the political process is to advance the black agenda, to advance black issues, to not forget black people, to not forget the substance from which we came."

McKinney provided an example of how she turned negatives into positives. "I have a percentage of rural white Georgia voters in my district. They didn't like me, either, because I was black and couldn't relate, or because I was a women and couldn't relate. Many of the farmers had trouble getting past one or two of those. So I ran as 'Why not a woman this time?' We were able to capitalize on the frustration that many of the voters felt. We took that negative and turned it into a positive."

As a result of her willingness to try to work through the concerns of all of her constituents, Cynthia won the resulting August runoff and became the Democratic congressional candidate. "After I became the nominee Pat Schroeder came down to Georgia and campaigned for me. You don't usually think of Georgia as her territory, but she came anyway."

Through her "unsung heroes," Cynthia went on to raise ten times more money for her campaign than her Republican opponent raised. "It was a Civil Rights struggle that put those unsung heroes in the community together through church networks, through NAACP networks, environmental networks—all of those unsung people who generally are looked down upon because they don't have very much and they fight out there singing a song that is against the chorus of the day. Those are the people who got behind me, and those are the people to whom I dedicate myself."

On election day, Cynthia became Georgia's first and only African American congresswoman by capturing 75 percent of the vote. "Our campaign victory was so phenomenal because we represented a different way to ascend the ladder, maybe in life, maybe just in politics. Our campaign theme was 'Warriors don't wear medals, they wear scars.' "

Cynthia entered the United States Congress on a high note but received the same disagreeable welcome as she had in the Georgia State Legislature. In the older white male kingdom, Cynthia stood out: a young, vibrant black woman wearing colorful flowing dresses and sneakers, her hair in two elaborate braids. And yet months after most freshmen were recognizable figures on Capitol Hill, Cynthia was still treated like a stranger. There had been the incident with the House elevator operator in February. A month later, a Capitol garage attendant suggested she was in the wrong place. And in August, a police officer grabbed her by the arm at a House metal detector that members are allowed to bypass.

Her fellow congressmen—and some congresswomen—weren't any warmer. A few minutes after she took a seat at her first meeting of a House Foreign Affairs subcommittee on Western Hemisphere Affairs, she realized that no one in the group was going to welcome her. She was the only woman present, and the men ignored her. When the committee members got up to have their picture taken, they did not include her. The meeting resumed with the chairman going through the agenda, addressing his fellow males. "I felt like Ralph Ellison's invisible man," McKinney told *Newsweek* in November of 1993.

The icy reception of her male colleagues did not dampen her fervor. Other congresswomen offered spirited, gutsy support to their younger sister. "Maxine Waters was the person who really opened the key to Congress for me. There is nobody in this world like her. Since I've been here, Pat Schroeder has also continued to be available whenever I need her help or advice. In fact, I feel I have a good relationship with all the women in Congress."

Cynthia continued to be as outspoken on Capitol Hill as she had been in the Georgia State Legislature. She supported universal health care, small-business development, and environmental regulations that protect the rights of minorities and the poor. She told reporters that her overriding issue was whether Americans can live together "with justice and fairness for everyone."

It seemed like an impossible task. Back in the Georgia State Legislature she had been somewhat successful in assembling the ninety-one votes needed to pass legislation. "We were always in a defensive mode trying to stave off unfair attacks on the black community, or on poor people, or on people of color or just on issues of right and wrong. We had to form coalitions to marshal votes. Sometimes we were successful, many times we were not.

"Up here in Congress, it's 218 votes that we have to fashion together by hook or by crook. It's a tremendous responsibility. At the same time, it does offer its rewards because we are successful on occasion. We are always trying."

One year after being interviewed for this book Cynthia's success story suddenly went wrong, showing how fragile a hold black women have on the reins of power. In 1995 Georgia's Eleventh District was ruled unconstitutional by the Supreme Court of the United States. However, once district lines are redrawn, McKinney will undoubtedly run again. There is every possibility that she will represent a new district in Congress, perhaps playing an even stronger hand than before.

Cynthia McKinney was not the only woman in the group to face the threat of defeat. No one could have been more prepared and more enthusiastic to accept a position of power than Dr. Josephine D. Davis, who in 1991 became president of York College, part of the City University of New York (CUNY) system. York College, with nearly seven thousand students, is located on a fifty-acre campus in Jamaica, New York, a city whose recent population reflects a wide ethnic mix.

Josephine was York's third president since its founding in 1966, and the first African American woman to be appointed to the presidency of a senior college in the CUNY system. By any measure, it was an impressive achievement.

Josephine D. Davis was a seasoned professional with impeccable credentials. She held a master's in mathematics from Notre Dame, and a doctorate of education in mathematics from Rutgers. She had taught for several years at graduate and undergraduate levels, followed by solid administrative experience as vice president for academic affairs at St. Cloud Technical College in Minnesota, where she directed on-campus programs and also developed international programs of study in England, France, Germany, China, Costa Rica, and Japan. She also served as dean of the Graduate School of Albany State College in Albany, Georgia, where she was named Woman of the Year in 1987 by a blue-ribbon panel of community leaders, the only African American to be so honored in that Deep South state.

In her hardworking career, Josephine had gathered an impressive list of honors, including the Kellogg Foundation National Fellowship Award and the National Science Foundation Academy Year Fellowship. She was a member of several national committees and advisory boards, and was noted for her special interests in international programs, minority and multicultural education programs, and science education. She was particularly interested in developing leadership among women and people of color.

The new appointment made Josephine an instant celebrity, and she got off to a rousing start. With all of her experience she should have known better than to underestimate the enormous resentment her appointment would regenerate.

Almost immediately she ran into trouble. The York College administration had been all-white for twenty years. "There were no blacks," said Josephine. "The system was very dictatorial, autocratic. Then here I come, democratic, and they accused me of being dictatorial."

A whisper campaign started among the faculty: Was Davis capable of running the institution?

"You always have to do more," she said. "You always have to prove yourself, you're always in their eyesight."

She did do more, much more. "My policy was sharing and inviting them to the table. They got resources and documents from me they'd never seen before. It was almost like a no-win situation. No matter what you do, you can't do enough."

Josephine also reached out to the culturally diverse population of Jamaica. "We invited schoolchildren to come in and we showed them traditions of different cultures around the world. I always talk to them about thinking ahead. My mission is to uplift the people."

Her outreach efforts continued to be resisted by some of the faculty. "Those who disagreed with me loved York the way it was. They wanted to stay inside the walls around the campus, don't let the community come in. They are a very few, but they are a vocal minority. The students, the community, everybody knows we're going in the right direction, except for those few."

After a year at the helm, Josephine had still not set the date of her inauguration as York's president. She wanted to design a ceremony that would express her vision of York's future. At this time she made another trip to Africa.

In Ghana, she met a university professor who was troubled by an impending choice he had to make. He was torn between his obligation to return to his village and accept the responsibility of being "enstooled" as their leader, or to continue his teaching life in the Western tradition. He chose to honor his commitment to his village. He invited Josephine to witness the ceremony.

This experience proved to be soul shaping. "To see this man transformed from the university to the village—to change from coat and tie to *kente* cloth and sandals, to majestically walk into his home and accept the responsibility of being enstooled—I realized that I, too, needed to prepare myself for a similar role."

In the West African culture, enstoolment is a serious matter. Nothing makes a clearer statement about your commitment to the people in your community. It requires a period of study and reflection, followed by a public vow unmatched by any other form of oath of office.

Josephine believed that an enstoolment ceremony would send a powerful message about her commitment to York College and her vision for its future in the context of its surrounding community. She intended for the ceremony to signal that under her administration everyone's unique cultural attributes would be valued and respected. She hoped that York College would become a global community.

Dressed in traditional African regalia, Josephine made her inaugural address in the school's auditorium before approximately 1,500 students, staff, faculty, and community leaders. Her speech emphasized the importance for York College to emerge as a leader in its "global neighborhood." Behind her as she spoke stood twenty students holding flags of the nations of their ancestry.

"York College is a welcomed and long-awaited solution to the southeastern Queens immigrant and minority population," she said.

"It was a beautiful celebration. We had all the kids from the high schools come, and they danced and sang and brought gifts. It went on from twelve noon to seven o'clock in the evening. We had an African bazaar. That signaled that we were going to be about cultural identification, and that the Western perspective was not necessarily going to be the dominant perspective any longer."

The backlash was immediate. Anonymous hate mail poured in. Packages of rotten meat were left on her doorstep. The enstoolment ceremony had pushed the "vocal minority" over the edge.

Josephine went about her business. Meanwhile, leaders of the faculty union at York accused her of being mean-spirited and incompetent. Generalized complaints were soon followed by rumors of fiscal mismanagement. There is nothing like money to attract media attention. Union leaders had finally found the spot guaranteed to draw public reaction, and they kept hammering away at it.

Josephine was accused of transferring funds from York's Adult and Continuing Education Division to the discretionary fund. Union officials also claimed that she had taken her husband and son on a trip to South Africa and billed the expenses to the college. (According to Dr. Davis, the money used for her husband's ticket was the same amount she was owed by the university for her own ticket. Instead of requesting her reimbursement, she purchased the ticket for her husband, viewing it as an "even wash.") They also said she spent more than $270,000 renovating her CUNY-owned, sixteen room home. Dr. Davis pointed out that expenditures, which had been approved by CUNY's Central Administration, included renovating and refurbishing the campus office complex to include a student lounge and faculty resource room.

From the beginning union leaders made their accusations public by giving quotes and writing letters to newspapers and professional journals. Complaints grew louder. Though attacks now seemed to come from many different sources, none were as unsettling as those launched by members of her own black faculty. A group calling itself Concerned Black Faculty and Staff circulated a position statement condemning her. It seems that they, too, were embarrassed by the enstoolment ceremony and resented Josephine being "crowned queen of the college and community." The letter sounded convincing. According to the unsigned letter, "any individual who dares to professionally disagree with, or question Dr. Davis' judgement is swiftly and severely dealt with in the harshest manner within her power."

Who—and how many—were behind the anonymous letter remains unknown. The individuals involved in Concerned Black Faculty and Staff never identified themselves, because the "sudden severance and other forms of retaliation make it difficult for many people to come forth at this time." According to one well-informed campus source, their numbers were few and no organized group was behind the letter. Dr. Davis said there were no black faculty members involved in the effort.

Josephine seemed to take it philosophically. "I'm changing the culture," she said. "We are going through a radical culture change, and the dissenters want to hold the culture." She herself believed that the faculty union leaders, whose power was being eroded by her changes, were behind the dissent. She felt certain that the majority of the faculty was behind her, and she was convinced that she had strong community and student support. But if this was true, it was not strong enough to protect her.

One must always question the role racial and gender biases may be playing in any dispute that involves black women. Efforts to undermine their leadership can come from almost anywhere and may be disguised. This is one reason why most blacks seldom criticize another black person, no matter how culpable an individual may appear on the surface. However, the rule does not always extend to black women. Certainly, it did not extend to Josephine Davis.

In February of 1995, a constantly embattled Josephine took a "leave of absence" to contemplate her future. During her tenure, enrollment increased from 3,500 to over 8,000 students and external funding increased by over 70 percent.

The presidency was assumed by Thomas K. Minter, a former dean at CUNY's Herbert H. Lehman College. In her absence, auditors began to review her past expenditures. She told newspaper reporters that she was confident that the audit would clear her of any financial wrongdoing. Several months later, the audit report was completed. As Josephine predicted, the auditors found nothing wrong.

Josephine Davis was interviewed for this book before she stepped down, when she still believed she could overcome. At the end of the interview, she was asked: "Where do you see yourself in another five years?" She answered, "Still in higher education policy making. Whether it's in South Africa, China—I have a well-developed global network."

She spoke lovingly of her husband and two grown daughters, both graduates of Spelman College. "He is my only husband," she said, "and he's African American. We commuted for ten years when I was in Texas and then when I was in Minnesota and our children were in Atlanta. He handles everything marvelously. He just says, 'Frankly, my dear . . .' My personal life is very satisfying and family centered."

The majority of black female leaders participating in this investigation have honed their survival skills to near perfection. However arduous their move into the power slot, their successes inspire us all. The key to their achievements seems to lie in their ability to assess reality, accurately recall how and why they sought their positions, and recognize the significance of their achievement. They never forget, not for a single moment, that they are black and female. One sister put it this way: "Every morning when I get up, I say to myself, 'I'm gonna show you, m——f——s, that I'm just as good as you are.' "

8

"Mama Never Said There'd Be Days Like This"

Stress is when you are away from home 65 percent of the time. Stress is even when you are home, you are 100 percent in the job, 365 days a year. Stress is when you desperately need some private time for yourself and your family, and you can't find it. Stress is when you're putting in fourteen, sixteen, eighteen hours a day, seven days a week. This week, I stayed here Friday night until eight-thirty, then took work home and worked Saturday and Sunday. Stress is when your husband feels that his competition is not another man, but the position you're in.

Tremendous satisfactions accompany the black female power experience, but power, especially Sister Power, has a significant downside. Fighting off relentless challenges to their leadership while trying to make over bankrupt systems creates enormous stress. Constant public exposure, isolation from everyday life, and marital breakdowns were additional stress factors. Many sisters who had successfully overcome racist and sexist obstacles on their way up, found they were unable to consistently externalize the many added pressures once they reached the top.

When they tried to describe the stress inherent in their roles, sisters spoke from the heart. "Your folks who have been with you for years, who see you in this job and think you have it all—you get to travel, you live in a nice place, you jet around in corporate planes, whatever the situation is—you can't go to them and say, 'I can't handle this. I'm scared.' They look at you and think, 'I would die for what you have! What are you complaining about?' I've had brothers say to me, 'You asked for it. You got it. And now you sit here and all you want to do is cry?' You just want to shake them and say, 'Why can't you see my pain and frustration?' "

They tried many stress-relieving solutions, including walking, talking, meditating, eating, shopping, and praying. These traditional methods helped to some degree but were by no means foolproof.

Even their greatest joys—managing multimillion-dollar budgets, six-figure salaries, and public recognition—created stress. Congresswoman Cynthia McKinney's comment was typical: "This job is nothing but stress, and the people around me have nothing but stress in their lives. When I enter the room, stress accompanies me, no matter what we're doing. That means that I can only have the best people around me. Anybody who can't deal with the stress is not someone I can afford to have around me."

The sisters were often isolated from the course of ordinary daily events, which created the burden of always being "on." Pamela Carter said, "I see myself as very human, but other people put you in a totally different spectrum. You cannot step outside of the dignity of the office. It's very isolated. People become intimidated, unnecessarily, or separate themselves from you. You have to work very hard to draw people toward you."

Mary Hatwood Futrell: "Sometimes people think you can perform miracles, you can solve every problem. It's not true. I'm human just like they are. But people don't look at me as Mary Futrell. They look at me as president of the NEA."

Reverend Willie Barrow agreed that it was lonely at the top: "People believe that 'now Reverend Barrow is the president of Operation PUSH and, my God, she is with Jesse Jackson, and could I call her? Would she go to dinner with me?' That is their perception. I don't feel that way. If somebody said, 'Let's have lunch,' I'll go have lunch. Then they say, 'Reverend Barrow had lunch with me,' or 'She talked to me personally on the phone.' I'm in awe that this is how I am perceived. To me, this is my ordinary job. This is what I do. It's nothing special."

If isolation was a leading stress factor, its flip side—public exposure—was just as bad. Whatever difficulties these famous sisters were struggling with were likely to become public issues. As one sister lamented, "I'm in the newspaper every day. The invasion of privacy is unrelenting. People scrutinize what you wear, how you walk, how you talk. I was not prepared for what goes along with being in such an influential role. The loss of that kind of privacy is most difficult."

They were often subjected to a double standard seldom applied to powerful men. Comments on their appearances—the color and style of clothing, the appropriateness of matching accessories, height, weight, and figure, and especially the style and length of hair—were part of every critique of their job performance. The media insisted on comparing these competent, sophisticated professional women to fashion models. The public could be even harsher.

Reverend Willie Barrow's unique style and vibrant manner of speaking were constantly criticized by some of her organization's own supporters. "Black women who came out of very high middle-class families, women who had double Ph.D.'s, and husbands and brothers who were this and that, criticized me. 'I don't think Reverend Barrow is a suitable leader. I don't think she dresses right.' They thought my grammar wasn't what it should have been, and I needed to change my tone. I was just criticized in every way. They never remembered that Fannie Lou Hamer, one of the greatest political leaders in this nation, couldn't read or write. They said that Harriet Tubman couldn't speak. But she spoke out of her heart, and when she did, everyone stopped and listened.

"They talked about my height so much that *Ebony* wrote an article on the effects of being short. They interviewed Sammy Davis and a whole group of short people. They interviewed me in the church, where I had to stand up on a little platform to speak."

The interesting thing about Willie Barrow's experience is that she never changed her style, but her critics eventually changed their attitude, primarily because she was simply too effective, too successful—too powerful—to continue to mess with. "These same people are now asking me to introduce them to people who can help them in their businesses. They want me to go to the negotiation table to speak for them, to hold a press conference for them, to come and speak at all of their meetings."

It's certainly striking that a significant number of Phenomenal women are prematurely forging their way into their grandmothers' dress sizes. This fact is not surprising, given that in every age range African American women are significantly more likely to be overweight than any other group. Roughly 26 percent of all Americans are overweight, and 12 percent are dangerously obese. Recent surveys by the Centers for Disease Control and Prevention report that obesity is rising among all minorities, and occurs most frequently among African American women between the ages of twenty-five and thirty-four. In their childbearing years (between twenty and forty-four) 35 percent of African American women are overweight, versus less than 25 percent of white women in the same age group. And by ages forty-five to fifty-five, fully half of all African American women are overweight.

Stress, fatty diets, cultural expectations, and possibly genetic endowment are presumed contributors. Power brokers of both sexes know that being overweight doesn't figure into the equation. (Excess weight reads as lack of self-control.) Further, these sisters knew that the visibility of big-bosomed sisters perpetuated the image of black women as mammies. As one said, "They'll all get mad at me for saying this, but we still play the role of mammy. That's how they see us, as mammies taking care of everyone in need."

They had the best intentions. Sisters said they tried to walk, jog, and dance away their weight. One woman replaced all of her living-room furniture with Nautilus equipment. Everyone wanted to eat nutritiously and exercise regularly, but found these difficult to achieve. Demanding work schedules, complicated by domestic responsibilities at home, left them with little time to concentrate on personal needs. Unlike Oprah Winfrey, none had yet been moved to hire a full-time cook and nutritionist to assume control of their diets.

The overwhelming stress often spilled into their private domains and wreaked havoc on their personal lives. Sisters were willing to discuss the more vulnerable aspects of their lives in order to offer insights to younger sisters starting out. For the most part, their intimate stories are off-the-record, their anonymity guaranteed. However, their comments are so insightful and useful that missing attributions cannot diminish their impact.

Phenomenal women have personal problems common to all successful women; a few, however, are unique to them, or at least magnified by the fact that they are black.

Powerful sisters continued to carry the major responsibility for maintaining their homes and caring for their children, husbands, and parents. Most said that motherhood was their most significant role. Pamela Carter described her two children, a twelve-year-old daughter and seventeen-year-old son, as her greatest achievements and the "joy of my life." Her opinion was shared by all. Children were more than "prized possessions." They anchored the women to the past, present, and future. These mothers were unwilling to sacrifice their parenting role in exchange for status and power, yet most found it impossible to do both jobs well at the same time.

What does a woman do with her children if she is sent to Congress? How often should she relocate her family while pursuing professional goals? At what age is it safe to leave her child in the care of others while she conducts the business of the people? And how do children respond to powerful mothers?

While the answers are unclear, the concern is ever present. One woman told about taking her son to a social function organized in her honor: "Everyone was congratulating me and telling me about my great achievement. And then I heard my son say, 'My mother can take care of everybody, except me.' I was devastated!"

Many chose to postpone career opportunities in order to attend to domestic responsibilities. Others asked those around them to make adjustments, negotiating trade-offs with their partners or helpers. "You get the kids off in the morning, I'll pick them up after school." Or "You stay home when the kids are sick." Some, in the tradition of the extended family, moved their mothers or mothers-in-law in with them to help fill domestic roles. And some, without apology, remained childless.

Domestic responsibilities did not necessarily ease up as children got older. "On one day, I shook hands with almost a thousand people. Then I got into a car, dashed to the airport, and flew to my daughter's graduation. Then we tried to have a little vacation, but I had to come back to settle some crisis. A few days later I was driving down south to help our other daughter move."

More than half of the sisters interviewed had children over eighteen. At least 30 percent had young children, from elementary school through junior and senior high school. Of the remaining group, some were stepmothers and some had never had children. At least 20 percent of the women now respond to the title "grandmama." In their grandchildren's eyes they are "grand" women.

A fertile area of investigation would be to examine the growing-up experiences of children who have publicly powerful mothers—through the eyes of those children when they are adults. Are their experiences similar to children who have powerful fathers? Are their growth and development stunted by constantly walking in their mothers' shadows? One CEO said: "My oldest son says, 'Mom, too much. Can't you let up?' Then he will say, 'Okay, I'll get on the bandwagon for today, but this is too much, I don't want it.' But I think my youngest son will end up being just like me."

Because power is such a relatively new phenomenon among women, we can only speculate on the outcome of motherly power. All of us shared the pain experienced by Dr. Joycelyn Elders when her son's difficulty with the criminal justice system became public. In addition to dealing with the pressures of a high-visibility job, Dr. Elders undoubtedly felt the sting of the public's perception that she was unable to raise a "productive, law-abiding citizen." In the minds of many, her son's predicament was her failure.

Whether we like it or not, women are held responsible for what goes on in the home. We are expected to raise the children, and raise them right. We also expect this of ourselves. But even when given the best of care, children sometimes choose the wrong path. Public exposure of a child's difficulties is emotionally devastating to both parent and child, and leads all mothers to reexamine the choices they made, or are making, when their children were young.

Some sisters whose jobs required long periods away from home left their children in the care of grandparents. Grandparents have always played an instrumental role in raising the next generation of black youth. However, many grandmothers today are young and still working, and not as likely to be at home in traditional roles, so this wasn't always an option.

Congresswoman Cynthia McKinney, a single mother with an eight-year-old son, has always been willing to speak publicly about how she resolved the dilemma of raising a young child alone while living among high-profile Washington politicians. She chose to let her son, Coy, a soccer and baseball buff, live with his grandparents in Atlanta, where he could have a more normal childhood growing up in an African American community.

Cynthia spends her workweek in Washington, and tries to be in Georgia every weekend. She handles these regular separations in a way that most powerful male politicians would probably never think of. Although she knows that her parents take loving care of Coy, McKinney keeps her finger on the pulse of his everyday life. When she is in Washington, she calls Atlanta each morning, checking to make sure that Coy is ready for school and knows her schedule. At night, she reviews his homework by fax; and, like most mothers, every now and then doles out punishments.

Cynthia McKinney does not consider this a negative lifestyle. "I walk in the shoes of many women," she told *Ebony* magazine in 1994. "I just happen to have a nontraditional job. . . . It makes me feel very happy that I've brought a young person into the world and that I'm fostering a sense of independence and social commitment. . . . I think he rolls with the punches much better than I do."

McKinney's situation illustrates that an independent, uncompromising African American woman needs support from her family and community if she is to resist being absorbed by the power experience. She cannot do it by herself.

Help can also come from sources outside of family and community. Every working woman knows the difficulties of trying to balance work with domestic roles and trying to do both well. Those with children must find proper child care. In addition, other help may be employed to relieve some of the household burden. The balancing issue intensifies considerably in the lives of sister-leaders. Women in top spots often find it impossible to find time to fill any domestic role at all.

Like the fictional character Ester, in Bebe Moore Campbell's *Brothers and Sisters*, powerful black women struggled with the decision to hire domestic help. Did hiring help mean they were becoming "Miss Ann"? Could they hire a "girl" to do the dirty housework and slip easily into the role of "Ma'am"? And who should they hire: Another sister? A Latina? Or a white woman?

In *Black Women Abolitionists*, Shirley Yee told a story about Sarah Douglass. While attending a Quaker meeting in New York in the early 1880s, Mrs. Douglass, wife of Frederick Douglass, was approached by a white woman who assumed she was a domestic servant. "Doest thee go a house cleaning?" the woman asked. Mrs. Douglass was outraged by the stereotypical image that all black women were domestic servants. More than one hundred years later, another example: a graduate of the University of Pennsylvania with a bachelor's degree in communications had moved to center-city Philadelphia in search of new professional opportunities. One evening, she was doing her laundry at the neighborhood Laundromat. As she was folding her blue laced-trimmed underwear, a middle-aged white woman popped her head in the door and asked, "How much do you charge?"

For the generation of black women whose memories are marked by images of their mothers and grandmothers working as domestic servants in white homes, hiring domestic help presented a conflict. Some absolutely refused to do it. "I clean my own toilets. I clean the toilet bowl. And why shouldn't I? I wonder about paying for my freedom with a low-wage job to another human being. And who would it be? Some poor little black woman. And I would be standing on her back. It's not as though I haven't tried it. But in the end, we decided it would be better if we did it ourselves."

"I clean my own house. It keeps you humble."

"No, I don't hire domestic help. But that's because my mama lives with us and takes care of the house. I'm not sure what I would do without my mama."

However, one does not have to sit in the power seat for long before realizing that domesticity does not merge comfortably with a power career. For some, employing others was seen as a positive solution. Several sisters emphasized that domestic work itself was not inherently demeaning; how it worked out depended largely on the nature of the employer-employee relationship.

Congresswoman Eva M. Clayton explained: "From time to time I have needed people to come in and do the work. I have no problem hiring domestic help. They're like members of my family."

Marcia Gillespie, editor in chief of *Ms.* magazine, expanded on this theme: "I knew that I needed help with the housework. That was one of the things that I was working for, the luxury of having someone clean the house. But I know some African American women have problems working for other African American women. So I asked my mother, who used to do this kind of work, 'Mom, do you think this would be okay?'

"She said, 'Girl, as messy as you can be I certainly hope so . . . absolutely so.' She said, 'This is honest work. My own mother did this kind of work and I was proud of my mother. You should know by now from hearing stories from me and your grandmother about how to be the right kind of employer.'

"What's important to me is mutual respect between worker and employer. I respect her work; she respects mine. You know what I mean? We do it. And Mrs. Evelyn Longmire, I thank you very, very much."

One sister described this special relationship with her housekeeper: "She is sort of like my mother and my grandmother. When I get home at night she is there, we can sit and have a class of wine together, and I can just pour my heart out. Half of the time I'm not sure she knows what I'm talking about, but she listens. And she's not going to let anyone talk about me. She's going to protect me. If I'm tired, she will turn down my bed or she'll draw my bath. You know, it's good to be home and to be with your mother. I also have a driver, who has become a very close friend. And a gardener. I need someone to take care of the lawn, too."

Ultimately, all of the women were forced to decide how to arrange this part of their lives. They made different choices, many with mixed feelings. The challenge rested in their ability to discover a comfortable space in the domestic trap zone.

If caring properly for beloved children and coping with household responsibilities contribute to a woman's stress load, husbands and lovers sometimes help reduce it—or make it even worse. Husbands played a potent role in the African American female power scenario. For some, love and support from husbands provided the emotional foundation that fueled their fighting spirits.

Pamela Carter, attorney general for the state of Indiana, described her husband's efforts to help her maintain her balance during a brutal election campaign: "I don't know that many men could have been supportive of me and my trek because it's a tough one. When I was running for office, he was attacked as viciously as I. And with just as much vitriol. So he had to withstand a great deal of scrutiny. Then we had to come home to an empty house, without hot food on the table. I have no complaints. He's a great guy."

Other happily married sisters talked about how they manage to work out the difficulties that their positions imposed on their marriages. One sister has been married for more than forty-five years. In the beginning, her husband wanted her to conform to a traditional domestic role. Over the years, wife and husband made many compromises and adjustments.

"We take separate vacations, because he can think and relate as his own person when he is away. When I'm away alone, I can be the person I want to be. Once, when a particular national crisis was on, he came home from vacation and I wasn't there. Eventually I got home, but then I had to stay on the phone all night. That was really painful. I apologized. I said, 'Honey, I'm so glad to see you. I know that I need to be talking to you and you need to be talking to me, but circumstances will just not allow us to do that.' The next morning, I got up at five-thirty and was cooking breakfast because I wanted to share part of me with him. He said, 'I don't want to eat at this hour.' I said, 'But this is the only time we have together, so why don't we be together. So, we ate together, and about 7 A.M. the phone started ringing again. Sometimes that's just the way it is."

Many women described themselves as feminists, but a few unexpectedly had more traditional views. After thirty-five years of marriage and more than a quarter century in the public arena, one sister described her happy marriage in the following manner:

"I have a positively unique relationship with my husband. I

follow the Bible as close as I can, and it does say that the man is the head of the house. The man is supposed to love the wife, but wives are supposed to submit themselves to the husband. I believe that you have to follow that book because it gives direction to life so things won't break down. Let's face it. God planned all this and he planned it well. He gave the women the charge, the responsibility, to bring forth life. That's why I say, you may not find a father at home, but you will always find a mother, even among the animals. God gave women those certain qualities that one would need to stay with that child and nurture.

"God gave us women the ability to get whatever we want from a man. I asked my husband before I took any of these positions, 'What do you think? It's up to you.' And I get the answer I want. He always encourages me. A lot of men aren't that secure. My husband is a very secure, strong man. Any woman that wants to be a leader, or wants to go run a business or go out into the professional world, has to make sure she marries a man that understands it. Otherwise, you are just going to have hell on earth.

"You have to be intelligent enough to observe a man first, and know that you can't change him! And too many men try to reshape the woman. It can't be done. My husband has never tried to inhibit me, but he does try to encourage me to do more. And he is proud. Many men come up to him and say, 'How in the world do you live with her? I couldn't handle it!' He tells them, 'I'm proud of her and delighted and I want to see her do more.' So I don't have the problems that many of my sisters have. I know it's been a horrendous, disturbing part of their lives."

She was right about that. Only 26 percent of the total group of women said they had stable, long-term first marriages. Many more spoke of tension-filled marriages. One sister's high-profile position led to constant fights with her husband, who tried to do her job from the bedroom. "My husband encouraged me to take the job and said he was proud of it, but on a day-to-day basis it was very difficult. Ninety percent of our arguments for five years were about how I was handling my job based on what he read in the newspapers or heard on television and around town. I used to tell the governor, 'If I can get out of the house in the morning, I can face anything anybody else says.' "

The husband of another high-profile sister refused to be seen with her in public. Her professional conferences, dinner meetings, fund-raising, and other social events were strictly solo occasions. "I remember being at one social gathering. Dinner had been served, the guest of honor saluted, and the space was being cleared on the dance floor. I knew I was expected to get things moving, but I didn't have a dance partner. The men, all of whom were my subordinates, didn't want to make an inappropriate move, and I was uncomfortable asking one of them for the first dance. Everyone was trying to be so professional. So, we all just stood around. It's funny, it was such an awkward moment. This was before the electric slide."

Another said, "I know it's been difficult for my husband. We're both fighters for racial freedoms. But my career, my success, overshadows him. On the other hand, his ability to understand gender issues is zero. I'm tired of the sexism that exists in the relationship. I'm tired of genuflecting to men. I want to make this relationship work, but I'm tired of doing it. I want a man who can enjoy who I am and what I've accomplished."

For several women, severe domestic rifts ultimately led to separation. Divorce and being single were commonplace.

One said, "I had a wonderful, extremely supportive husband. Then he said something one day. He said, 'I have no problems with what you do, as long as you don't make any more money than I.' And that's when it started to fall apart. Because, how do you control your income? He was trying to compete where he couldn't compete. He couldn't understand that my excess in terms of salary could go all the way to the top. I was willing to have it go to the top . . . put the frosting on the cake. I said, 'You know, this is a way we can take these winter vacations, this is a way to get all the things we want.' It got so he couldn't enjoy it. He turned to booze. He just couldn't deal with it."

Others agreed that the higher they rose in their careers, the greater the pressure on their marriages. One said, "I didn't see the support waning until the latter stages of my career, when I became more successful. Then we seemed to grow apart. He was a very intelligent man, but I guess his macho or whatever was taking over, and men probably teased him, calling him 'Mr. (Jane Doe).'

"My salary was a lot more than his, which may have had a lot to do with it. But it wasn't the whole story. The way I handled my finances was not to show the difference. We deposited our checks into the same account and took money out for our own weekly expenses and whatever we needed. It wasn't as though I brought my check home to him. I even used direct deposit. There were no psychological reminders of how much I made, and I never kept him up-to-date. If I got a raise, it just went right into the account, included as part of the family fund. I paid the bills and we lived off of what was left. I think it was my visibility that affected him more than anything else."

Role switching was common. "I was interested in politics and I married a person who was interested in pursuing political objectives. As it turned out, I had more ambition for him than he had for himself. At that time, I never thought that I would be the one. I considered myself his support staff. My dad said, 'You don't have to be support staff. You could be the one.' It all began for me there. The marriage was over."

One woman described a different way in which power interferes with marriage: "My husband met me as a professional. He saw the person who could walk into a room of ten thousand people and never bat an eyelash. Who could breeze in and out of the White House and interact with the president and those kinds of folks and never become the least bit ruffled. Could go and sit down and talk to any CEO and plead a case on an issue. I could walk into a community meeting where there were thousands of people ready to strangle me and still be okay. That's the person he met, and the strength he sought. Unfortunately, he could never see the other side of a very complex person. The other side is that little girl who is scared to death, who some days doesn't know if she's going to get from point A to point B. Who just needs to be held. Who wants to sit and cry—and then walk out of the room and kick ass."

While 68 percent of the total group of women had been divorced, 37 percent of the divorced women found marital happiness in a second marriage.

One sister was philosophic about the breakup of her first marriage and felt she learned an important lesson about herself. "My first husband was a wonderful man, but we had different values and wanted to go in different directions. I was absolutely devoted to my career. Actually, he was the healthier of the two of us because he was dedicated to having a whole life. My second husband is as much a workaholic as I am. He's inching toward getting a life, so I've got to start inching toward getting a life, too, so I'm not left behind like I was the first time."

In most instances, first marriages occurred before the women had grown into themselves and before their careers began to rise. A sister now in her late thirties said, "I was married the first time at eighteen, through four years of undergraduate school. He was eight years older. Nice guy. I bent over backward to make him happy, and didn't think of what it took to make me happy. I went to night school one year so I could work full-time during the day so he could buy a new car. I couldn't even drive. I couldn't sign on the checking account. I don't blame him, I blame myself.

"Between the ages of eighteen and twenty-two I changed a lot. People who know me now cannot believe that I could have been married to somebody who did not allow me access to the money I earned. I outgrew my husband. Then I was single for four years.

"Before I married the first time, I had never washed a load of clothes nor had I cooked anything. I had never even thought about doing those things. My mother always said that housework was not her long suit. She was good at other things, so she never placed a very high priority on that. I tried, but I was never very good at filling the traditional domestic part.

"I am more domestic in my second marriage. The first time my mother visited me here she saw me washing some walls and she said, 'How did you learn how to do that? And why?' "

Second marriages usually came much later, when the women were already reaching the top; the second time around they made sure that they chose men who were comfortable with strong, successful women. One described the new experience this way: "When I met my second husband, he said he knew I was a rising star and he wanted to be associated with me. He's a man of accomplishment and he was secure about himself. He has exposed me to things that I would have never been exposed to. He makes a contribution to whatever I do, and I respect his opinion. So we are a team. That has a lot to do with the kind of respect, the kind of partnership, the kind of relationship, someone like me needs. We've been married a long time now. How should I say it . . . we're on the same mature social level."

Some sisters are still looking for a few good men, but Census Bureau statistics are not encouraging. Whether they are divorced or never married, black women spend more time being single than any other racial or gender group. In sheer numbers, there are over one million more black women than black men. Many of these sisters were over forty, and in that age group the eligibility pool of brothers was rapidly dwindling. Black men continue to have the shortest life expectancy (60.0 years) among all groups. Higher rates of homicide, incarceration, drug abuse, and other social assaults further reduce the supply of eligible mates. And not every single black male can be viewed as "good marriage material" for a powerful black woman. Private desires and public expectations are often an uneasy fit. Speaking of a new potential boyfriend, one sister reluctantly said, "He's super special in many ways, but it's almost like I have to keep him in the closet."

Another added, "You could get real lonely if you're waiting for a strong black man to come to you and say, 'I think you're the one I need to be with.' "

As one sister bluntly put it: "There ain't no brothers no where, no how. I mean, I don't know where they are and if you know where they are, please send me a note."

Their situation is in sharp contrast to the experiences of most powerful men, who attract more than a fair share of female admirers. When it comes to men, power is more potent than good looks and kind deeds. Powerful men often tell stories of aggressive females in hot pursuit showing up at social and political gatherings, staking out their territory, and hunting down their prey. Powerful men receive women's room keys and pieces of underwear, as well as seductive messages by letter, telephone, or E-mail. Some are too committed to their wives and remain untempted, but the resistance factor of others appears limited.

Powerful women tell different stories. Potential mates are much less willing to throw themselves on the female's power altar. The women were fully aware of the differences between their own romantic lives and those of their male counterparts.

Developing a social life that is congruent with an overpowering public persona is tough. Old friends disappear and new ones are hard to find. "People who were my friends, people who I thought we were all on the same wavelength—we would have our rap sessions until two in the morning, discussions about how we were going to change the world, that kind of thing—they decided to leave me behind. One young man told me that he wasn't good enough. I thought he was fine, I was proud to be with him. But he told me he wasn't good enough."

Another sister was more concise: "I get a lot of respect, but the guys don't hit on me."

Sisters were blunt on this issue. "It has been very hairy socially, as far as my romantic life is concerned. I think I'm intimidating. I think it's hard for men to approach me. I've been told that. Many times the way you meet people is in your public persona, which is bigger than life. It's difficult to find secure, strong African American men who do not feel threatened by strong African American women. Some feel, and perhaps they have the right to feel that way, that we have taken some of their places—the places they have the right to hold. It's tough. When I've tried to compromise who I am, it doesn't work well. Right now, I would say that my social life is a C–."

"All of my men serve three-month terms," said another sister. "That's about as long as they can stand going out with a powerful black woman."

One young woman looked around and wondered if she would ever have a man in her life at all. "It's a scary thing. Everyone I know seems to be single. Does that mean that black women with power must give up their romantic lives?" Some did decide to forget about having a permanent relationship with one man, but they did not necessarily give up on romance. With caution, one particularly resourceful woman opted for five freestanding relationships, each fulfilling different needs.

Another said she chose to put her children and career ahead of looking for a second husband: "I don't think I have time for one man. I can have several men in my life, and I can have them when I want them. I couldn't go with a white man. That doesn't work for me. They're nice, and one wanted to marry me, but—I just feel very comfortable with a black man."

For some African American women, however, white men were an option. Six of the sisters had made this choice. Three of these, who had married white during the peak of the Civil Rights movement, were later divorced. Statistical analysis shows that in the seventies and eighties, marriages between blacks and whites increased threefold over a twenty-year period. These marriages were overwhelmingly black men to white women. More recently, the trend toward interracial marriages has included more marriages between black women and white men. In this investigation the sisters married to white men said they did not prechoose these relationships. According to one, falling in love just happened naturally:

"I'm troubled about all the conflict between black men and black women. I had a fabulous father who was a black man. I have a fabulous brother who's a black man. I have lots of friends who are black men. I certainly did not go out and seek my husband because he's a white man. I was in an airport, and he started talking to me, and I started talking to him, and the next thing I knew, we were married!"

Regardless of their current marital status, the sisters had all gained a practical wisdom regarding men. Basically, they repeated the solid advice offered to us by our own mothers and grandmothers: "If you want your relationship to work, you should marry your best friend. Someone who will continue to like you when the hot period is over."

Others cautioned, "If you want to keep working, you have to marry a man who doesn't feel threatened by your job. Look for a man who has a mother who has been happy working. She might have had to work, but she should have been happy doing it. I think younger black men are much more programmed to accept women working than older black men. If you want to stay in a career, if you want to combine it with family, you have to talk to your husband about what you want to do. I don't know one single black woman—well, maybe I know two, but I wouldn't brag about them—who has not had a family and worked at the same time. Black women just do it."

One sister emphasized that the issues involved were complex: "I'm very quick to say to young professional women, if you're getting married that's fine, but you have to define your own space. You have to force a partnership, because otherwise you will suffer. Your professional career will suffer, your family will suffer. I'm a big advocate for individual therapy, especially for professional women, because the number of balls we keep in the air is incredible."

One divorced sister who said she might remarry knew she

would have to find a particular kind of man: "It would have to be a relationship with mutual trust—a relationship where you like each other. Women have to ask real serious questions about marriage. Is this going to make sense? We cannot sell ourselves short."

Whenever she felt serious about a particular man, she consciously referred to a series of questions she kept posted above her bed:

" 'Do you want to make up this bed every day? Do you want to get up and make breakfast for somebody? Do you want to wash clothes? And do you want to give up half of your day every weekend or every day taking care of the house?' At the bottom of the list it says, 'If you answer no, you are not ready for a relationship.'

"So, every once in a while, when I get sucked into those things, I ask myself those questions with that particular guy in mind. Nah, you know, forget it. That is how I handle that."

One sister gave this final, universal advice: "Never subordinate your goals to those of a man. We have talent and we have a calling, each of us. Whatever that calling is, whatever those talents are, we need to use them. By using them well, we become a stronger community. And we become strong in our relationships because we are the best that we can be."

All of the women said that when it came to finding solutions to the multitude of stress-related problems, they were isolated. One said: "I wish somebody had sat down and said, 'Listen, you're going into this job, these are the ways you have to adjust yourself. You have to change your hairstyle, you've got to change this and that, and you've got to tell your husband what to expect.' Nobody said that to me. I was on my own."

Once again, without role models to advise them, their unique situation demanded creative thinking. They experimented with many different solutions, and the special insights they found can serve all women and men struggling to balance their lives.

Overcoming isolation was at the top of the list. Feeling isolated is an inevitable consequence of all leadership positions, regardless of the leader's race or gender. Powerful African American women had some surefire methods to reduce this particular kind of stress. They overcame loneliness by maintaining close and continuing relationships with their families, particularly their parents. Phenomenal women, no matter how high they fly, grab every available opportunity to visit the homestead.

Marcia Gillespie said she receives the same level of affirmation and support from her family now as she did when she was a child. "That's my safety mat."

One young sister, accustomed to directing folks to their proper tasks and giving out orders on a daily basis, sometimes made the mistake of taking this behavior home with her. Whenever she started directing traffic at home, her family chided, "Go outside and check the address on the front door! You're not up at the statehouse now." The good-natured teasing was enough to remind her to switch hats immediately.

Looking back on her long road to the top of the banking industry, Emma Chappell, who had lost her mother when she was still a child, said: "What really stabilized me is my family—my father and brother and sister. And now my children. I go home and might not come out for the entire weekend. It is not that I am doing anything, just catching up on some reading or relaxing with my daughters. They help me cook and we talk about everything, whatever is going on in our lives at that particular time. I help them through, and they help me through. When I do finally come out of the house, I am straight for the upcoming week."

This periodic reality check was important, given that most of these women were living a lifestyle that could easily detach them from the vast majority of the population. During periods of uncertainty, sisters went home to loving, supportive arms.

Maxine Waters, who is at ease with her congressional colleagues and with the president of the United States, also maintains her close connections to the people on the streets and folks in the neighborhood. "Power positions don't have to change you in ways that deny who you really are and where you came from," she said. "I maintain old friendships. I do what I have to do, and yet I can go back to the 'hood and live in it."

But family and old neighborhoods alone are not enough to sustain women who spend most of their time working all over the globe. All of the Phenomenal women said that finding sanity networks among their own age group was essential to being able to withstand the stress built into the power territory. "For the longest time I felt like I had to do it all alone. I didn't know where the support was. You don't outgrow old friends and family in terms of love, but you may outgrow them in terms of their ability to understand some of the challenges you're going through. When you need support, there's no place to go for it. That's where I was a year or two ago.

"A lot of things were happening in corporate America. A lot of us had been challenged. One day I met a sister on a plane. We were both flying to D.C. It wasn't a big deal, but we talked. Somehow, through the power of the spirit, she saw that I was at a particularly challenging point in my life. The next thing I knew, I was getting phone calls from sisters saying, 'Are you okay?' Or, 'Let's go to lunch.' It was a network of support that said, 'We are there for you, just open up and allow us to be there for you.' "

Their closest friends were seldom professional colleagues: "The numbers of professional peers are too few, the schedules are too crazy," said Pamela Carter. Although Pamela said she received support from other attorney generals, none are African American or females.

Many looked for ways to retain their ties with other sisters, finding that these relationships were the glue that held everything together. According to one, "There are times when you just have to leave all this power bullshit alone. I have a network of best girlfriends: one in Philadelphia, one in the District, and several in LA.

We can just get on the phone and talk about black men, talk about hairstyles, and talk about what really matters."

In the stress that comes from isolation and the constant struggle to gain ground, the African American sisterhood offers special qualities for Phenomenal women. Several of them say that black women provide a safe haven to discuss any and all matters related to the job and to the heart. "When I want to escape, I call some friends and go sit down and talk. I have gone to see friends and they've gotten out the pots and pans and started cooking and we sit there in the kitchen and we just talk, talk, and talk, and the next thing you know, I might have spent the night or something."

"When I can't take it anymore, when I need *it,* I go with black women because they'll take you in, they will nurture you, they will support you. Then they will kick your butt back out. Kick your butt right back into the world. Often I'll feel like my cup is empty, but after I meet with sisters my cup is renewed. Even with all the infighting and crappy mess, it feels good to be with black women. These are my people. They see it like I do."

Another CEO added, "Part of this networking among sisters is just to get together and holler about stuff. You say, 'This shit is ridiculous,' and everybody understands all the layers that encompasses. There's that reservoir that's almost like your blood or your genetic code, something inside of us that helps us keep our identity."

A well-known politician shared this vivid recollection: "One thing that happened when I first decided to run for office was very edifying for me. Black women in town were very active in the Political Action Program. Every Saturday we used to have what we called a 'critique,' all right? When I was planning to run for the council, they would come to my house. This was two to three years *before* the election, and they would critique my presentation.

"Now, I'll tell you one thing. If you want to have the epitome of criticism, get five or six black women in. They would come to my house, and I dreaded the hour, believe me, I dreaded the hour. But I needed it, because I was going to expose myself to the whole city, and these black women were there to help."

In the early stage of their careers, some sisters chose to distance themselves from the "bitchiness" of the "I-don't-like-your-looks" focus that characterized some black women's groups. Those who turned away sought other friendships among their professional colleagues, but socializing with white males for the most part proved to be unrewarding. They missed their sisters and found themselves searching for ways to reconnect to them.

Many sisters said they are now finding new joy in various women's service clubs such as the Jack and Jills and the Continentals, and sororities such as Alpha Kappa Alpha, Delta Sigma Theta, and Zeta Phi Beta. Working together with other sisters toward meeting important social and service agendas has become a powerful renewal mechanism that sometimes carries over onto the battlefield.

Mary Hatwood Futrell talked about the special role Delta Sigma Theta continues to play in her life: "Through all of the fifteen years I was emerging as a leader at the NEA, the Deltas were always networking, getting the word out. When I ran for local president they networked to make sure that people knew I was running. When I ran for state president they sent the word out that a Delta was running and needed support. Even when I ran as national secretary-treasurer, and then later as national president, they sent the word out. Everything from being a contact or raising money to being there when I needed them.

"There are others, too. Even people you don't think could possibly be paying attention provide support. You wouldn't think that Coretta Scott King, with all the things that she has to do, has time to pay attention to what's going on with me. But every once in a while I get a little note of advice. I get the same thing from Jesse Jackson, a little note of support. They say things like, 'I just want to know how you're doing. I know that things are kind of rough.' When you are maybe down, you get a note of support, 'You're doing a good job, hang in there.' "

Marcia Gillespie was one of the sisters who has been able to establish a widespread network of support among professional peers and personal friends, who often overlapped. "I have a powerful circle of friendships I have worked on, and it goes in many different directions. It starts with sisters, and goes on from there." As editor in chief of *Ms.* a significant part of Marcia's agenda is to bring together all sisters of every age and every color. She represents a new breed of sisters who have successfully developed trusting, equitable relationships with white women.

In addition to her sorority sisters Mary Hatwood Futrell also had discovered a wider support network. "You have a very close group—friends, family, colleagues, staff people—but that network can be much, much broader. Like the members of this organization, some people are a base of constant support, not in just day-to-day activities but support for me as a person. There are others out there who provide encouragement, telling you to stick to it, to keep going. The pleasant side of this job is when you get that kind of support and you don't expect it."

Pamela Carter's experience provided a prime example of finding personal support in unexpected places. Two short years into office Pamela discovered that she had breast cancer. Treatment included a mastectomy and chemotherapy. She was surprised and moved by an outpouring of public support.

"I don't think that I knew how much people were ready to befriend me," she said. "People can rally around you, not just as a public official, but as a human being." One local editorial commented at the time: "There are times in life that serve as reminders that power positions and politics really are not so important, and that everyone shares the common bond of humanity."

Because of her high visibility Pamela seized the opportunity to encourage other women to seek early cancer detection through mammograms and self-examination.

The experience also reminded her how satisfied she was with her life. Pamela had succeeded in striking a happy balance between her professional aspirations and her personal life, an accomplishment that all Phenomenal women strive for.

In some very special ways, powerful sisters looked for and discovered unique ways to relieve stress. They do not live in rose gardens, but they know how to find the support they need when they need it. They maintain ties to their families and childhood communities, take care of their children, make an effort to establish equitable relationships with staff, volunteer, and domestic help, join social and professional organizations where they can develop trusting relationships among their peers, and recognize that they often have a broader network of support in the world than they expected. Above all, with other sisters they engage in kitchen table dialogue, wrap themselves in oral tradition, reinforce cultural nuances, and share personal intimacies. And they pray—alone and together, they pray.

9

We've Come This Far by Faith

Sometimes I get into very hostile groups who are against what I am saying. I always go home and pray first, and always read a psalm before I speak to them, and somehow I feel some peace.

—*Dr. Dorothy Harris*
Former president,
National Association of Social Workers

The power of the spirit fuels Phenomenal women. Their faith in their mission and their faith in God appear unshakable. As with other important themes, their spiritual fervor also developed from the special content and context of their lives. Keeping the faith, believing in " 'da Lawd," and praying for relief from oppression has been a constant and central theme of the black community in America. At the same time, their American church upbringing fused with a deeper stream. In the African American community church, training is reinforced with stories of people "knowing things" and "feeling things," of receiving warnings and messages from those long gone from the face of this earth. God was present. The ancestral spirits were present. The unique blending of traditional and nontraditional beliefs imbues the black community with feelings of specialness. They are not just God's people, but people who are in tune and in touch with nature as well.

The sisters' stories of faith begin in childhood. All were raised up in one church or another, from Baptist to Presbyterian to Catholic to Hebrew. They attended Sunday school, morning worship, afternoon sessions, and evening prayer meetings. Their faith was nurtured by attending Baptist, Methodist, and Christian youth organizations and joining youth gospel choirs.

Unita Blackwell said her religious training was "in and out of the church, and people learned to do what was right and what was decent. When I was growing up, people took care of one another. They felt that was a religious act. You be nice to people, be respectful. God wants you to be good. We were Baptist, everything around us was Baptist, mostly. We attended what people used to call sanctified churches. There were also some Methodist churches. I am a Baptist, still am. I came up with the women around me, we went to church."

Emma Chappell proudly proclaimed, "I was raised in the church. I have never changed from Zion Baptist Church, not since the day I was brought into this world. It is probably very unusual for people in my profession to talk about it, but I feel that much of my success is owed to my church roots, and the fact that when I reach a period when I am under stress on the job, or just having a difficult time, I can come to church. I can sit down with my pastor and talk with him. This has been my founding grace. If anything has saved me, it has been that. Just listening to a good sermon and some good music seems to be all I need to help me cope."

As the sisters charted new paths, they continued to use their faith for support, but its expression began to take on new dimensions. Unita Blackwell remembered: "When we were raised up, everybody said, 'You got a good religion.' Then I went to finding out that religious people have killed in the name of their religion. You can make a religion out of anything. But if you've got the spirit of God in you, that's different."

Several other sisters became uncomfortable with the contradictions they observed in organized religion. Marcia Gillespie told about the time her pastor ridiculed a pregnant teenager in front of the whole Sunday morning congregation. Other clearly presented examples came from the Catholic women.

Paula Banks, head of the Sears Foundation, specifically remembered when her divorced mother wanted to remarry. Paula was about fourteen years old. "The church said that unless my mother could get an annulment from my father, that she would be excommunicated and would spend her eternal life in hell. I could not accept that. Not *my* mother. Who are Catholics to make those kinds of decisions for this good and caring God? But, still, I continued to practice my religion. I even went to mass every day when I was in college."

Paula confronted another unexpected, unpleasant reality after she graduated from college. "I wanted to be a schoolteacher. I went to the archdiocese because Catholic schools don't have the same kind of qualification restrictions that the public school system does. Suddenly, I was teaching math at an inner-city Catholic school. I taught fifth through eighth grade math. I learned a lot of things that year. This school was right on the border of the haves and the have-nots. Parents struggled to pay the school tuition. And the principal referred to my students as 'monkeys.' I went through a serious personal metamorphosis that year. Up until that point, I had truly believed that if you had dedicated your life to Catholicism and Christ, that meant you viewed people as being equal. I recognized the amount of prejudice and bigotry in that school and in that church, in a community that was all African American. It was appalling. For the first time in my life, I became radical."

Congresswoman Cynthia McKinney discovered that the liberation ideals to which she dedicates her life did not readily conform to church teaching. "I spent my formative years in the Catholic church. I always heard there was a difference between what people said and what people did. There was a lot of that in the Church.

While I admire the pope and that kind of thing, it is difficult for me to buy into the status of women, the strictness as far as contraception. How can this man who has never lived a moment in the real world—how can he talk to me, struggling in the real world? It's that kind of thing."

The women who were raised in a specific religion but no longer attend church services gave various reasons: Contradictions in church doctrine, oppression of women, racial prejudice, hypocritical behavior, and lack of role models for people of color and women. These are reasons similar to those given by other contemporary women, regardless of race.

If they sometimes left their churches behind, they always carried with them a spirituality independent of any organized religion. Cynthia McKinney said that she appreciated her religious upbringing, but she now attends all the different churches in her congressional district. "To the extent that the human spirit is what delivers us and keeps us going, I would say that I'm spiritual."

Unita Blackwell spoke of her intimate connection to a higher power. "I am a person who knows God from experience. I feel his spirit. Not from a standpoint of being so righteous that I ain't no good. I'm talking about his spirit guides me. I've had personal experiences that make me accept that spirit within me. Numerous times I've experienced my life on the line. In the sixties I struggled with the idea of religion. Why did God do it this way? Then I went to understanding, over these years, him saving me from the Ku Klux, and everything else. Getting me through these things. I had a spiritual development. Whether you're Muslim, Jew, or Gentile, God is bigger than any sect. So I'm a spiritual person."

As a whole, Phenomenal women accepted themselves as deeply spiritual beings and understood the essence of the larger natural order of things. Paula Banks said she believed that most black women shared a connectedness with a spirit that is beyond themselves. "I wake up every day and say, 'Thank you, Father.' Whether you are a Buddhist, or a Christian, or a Jew, there is something about African American women that says we know our strength and our power comes from someplace else. We work harder, we try more. But when all is said and done, I don't walk into any meeting without saying, 'Father, have me do what you would have me do. Make this opportunity what you want it to be, so in the end, I will have done what you would have me to do—for your power and your glory.' I think that there's a spirituality that connects strong African American women."

In fact, theirs had never been a Sunday-morning spirituality put on for churchgoing. Instead, from the beginning it was a spirituality that seemed to reach back to and encompass their African roots. All of the Phenomenal women seemed to participate in an undefined ethic that embraced the world community. Aretha Franklin sings about "Spirits in the Dark." Here were Spirit Women who relied on their ancestors and their strong faith in God to see them through.

Accepting the presence of spirits is not unique to these sisters, but it is a unique cultural aspect of the African worldview. A "worldview" is a system of thought integrating values, philosophy, behavior, and the perception of one's place in the world. The Western or European worldview tends to define the world by examining its visible, segmented components.

The Eastern or African worldview tends to define life in a circular, holistic fashion, where everything is felt to be interconnected. In this kingdom everything is alive, and ancestral spirits live in all objects. (This perception is based on the West African concept of animism.)

Western concepts that see individuals as self-generating, independent units are difficult to comprehend if you hold the Eastern worldview. In the Eastern view the individual self expands to include all of the ancestors, and even the yet unborn, all of nature, and the entire community.

The *African American* worldview shares elements of both the Eastern and Western concepts. Separation of church from government provides oppressed people with a safety zone. The pragmatic emphasis of traditional churches in American communities offers African Americans stability, as well as a base of operations from which they can reach into mainstream society and effectively work for change. At the same time, these Western church practices are dominated by the Eastern belief in spiritual forces. Black folks, regardless of their religion or church background, place great emphasis on destiny, "vibes," symbolism, and imagery. African American culture encourages people to move with the natural rhythm, to "go with the flow," to allow things to happen at the appropriate time. And time is always relative.

Accepting the expanded definition of self bridges the gap between the two streams of thought by encouraging responsibility to the community. In this context, a striking difference appears between Phenomenal women and Potentiates: in the interviews with Potentiates, there were constant *I*'s and *me*'s. By contrast *we* and *our* dominated the interviews of Phenomenal women, expressed in terms of the collective struggle and achievement of African American people.

Their profound spirituality accompanied black women as they joined the American power elite. They continued to draw on it to remain steadfast and committed to their purpose. The spirits of their African and African American ancestors, past and present—from Hatshepsut and Amina to Ann Nzinga and Yaa Asantewa, from Sojourner Truth and Harriet Tubman to Ida B. Wells-Barnett and Mary McLeod Bethune—were present in every interview.

The established powers that be don't always know how to adjust to these spiritually centered women. C. Delores Tucker spoke of one early career experience when she had been scapegoated and had been accused of mismanagement and abuse of public office. The press had a field day suggesting that she, the "new voice in government," had been corrupted by power. Tucker entered the meeting where the governor and her white male colleagues had gathered to call her to account and ultimately fire her. Before the meeting began, she invited the men to pray with her. The obvious sincerity of her request threw them completely off center. Having lost some of their armor, the governor and other cabinet members found themselves unable to stick to their agenda, and the attack on her competence couldn't move forward. C. Delores Tucker was not fired that day.

Roberta Palm Bradley, the executive from Pacific Gas & Electric, always carries a notebook to organize her day-to-day activities. Inside, in her handwriting, is this sentence: *There can be no crown without the Cross.* "I keep it with me at all times," she said. "It's a kind of touchstone for when things get rough. When I'm in a meeting, or dealing with a very difficult situation, I flip open that notebook and there's that quote."

Spiritual connectedness was universal among the group. Marcia Gillespie said her awareness of the spirits was always operating. "I believe it has kept me from tipping in the wrong direction, or totally flipping out. It reminds me of purpose, my purpose for being here, my relationships to others in the stream. It gives my sense of being a different meaning. It provides the mission and the meaning. I call on them when I'm feeling low and ask that they give me strength. I find great strength in stopping and considering what our ancestors faced. I hear them saying, 'And what are you complaining about, child?' Even though I know I still have a right to complain, and I will, they put things into proper perspective."

Many women described a similar habit of talking directly to their ancestors. When interviewed, one CEO was struggling to come to terms with the fallout from a hostile takeover of her firm by a major conglomerate. In the process of consolidating and restructuring, she knew people would be fired and that some lives would be devastated by the economic blow. She isolated herself and talked to her models of inspirations and to her departed ancestors. She said that the sense of connectedness with her family, both living and dead, was a great source of strength to her, helping her to maintain her equilibrium and lessening her isolation. She would eventually make the tough decisions, do what she had to do, but not before she had completed a thorough soul-searching.

Pamela Carter said that whenever she had a lot of difficulties, she could "always turn in, and it always worked." When asked if she heard inner voices, she laughed: "Mine have always been very active inner voices! In fact, I probably would never have passed those psychological profile tests they give you. 'Do you hear voices?' 'Oh, yes. I do hear voices.' "

Having active inner dialogues with spiritual forces was a constant source of support. They plugged it into the social and political realities represented on their interactive psychological "grid." From their youth, black women leaders had been using the grid to analyze problems in their proper context. Most said that when something went wrong they didn't immediately blame themselves; instead, they tried to identify the causes behind the situation. If, after analysis, a problem did turn out to be their own fault, they accepted the responsibility and got on with it.

With experience and maturity, the grid had expanded as new information was added to the free-floating arenas. The personal-support arena had been strengthened by educational and career achievements, mastery of various skills, new loved ones born into the family, and a heightened self-awareness. Their environmental supports had grown to include the care and nurturing of the larger community, social activism, new and lasting peer relationships, and the opportunity to pick up the torch and carry the legacy forward.

Constraints had also grown. Personal constraints might now include premature or inappropriate marriages and partnerships, and overwhelming domestic responsibilities. An uncontrollable ego also surfaced from time to time.

Environmental constraints became more tangible. Racism and sexism had a face, wore a suit, and were located in office buildings. Hostility was "in your face," and competition and resentment came from every corner. Policies and programs designed to wipe out hard-won gains were being implemented.

Through internal dialogues with their ancestors they could explore the interactive grid without anxiety, fix on the cause of an immediate problem, and examine possible solutions.

Looking to God, acknowledging the presence of the spirit, and listening to inner voices played a significant part in the way Phenomenal women handled stress and the pressures of public life. They created a spiritual buffer zone forceful enough to permeate every aspect of their social and personal lives. Spirituality is the foundation from which they mount their daily struggle. Their ability to tap into this greater power provides focus, direction, and inspiration. Faith is a constant companion, and these women never leave home without it.

10

Sister Power

> My style is empowering others to do things. I see myself as being the person who can convene things, and intervene, and bring people together to solve problems. I'm out front in a professional, humanitarian way. I am not trying to embarrass anyone or belittle anyone. I don't lead by pulling someone else down.
>
> —*Congresswoman Carrie P. Meek (D-Fla.)*

Phenomenal women are in the process of creating a new leadership model that has several distinguishing characteristics, including an unusual perception of power, decision making through consensus building, hard work, tenacious drive, and a willingness to break the rules.

Many feminist scholars have observed that women seem to have a different perception of the world, and a different way of wielding power. Maxine Waters talked about the difference between the way most men and most women exercise power. "If I can generalize, I believe that most women have a different way of approaching problems. Women are more up front in declaring our feelings. Men tend to lie to each other more about what they think and feel. They walk around, working with each other and hating each other at the same time.

"Even though it's true that women sometimes dislike intensely, I think we have a way of saying it to each other, and getting over it a little better. Men don't say it to each other, and they never get over it. They tend to hide behind the issue, rather than deal with the individual.

"The racists in the House can't tell me straight out that they're uncomfortable with me because I'm a black woman. Instead, they do what they did today, when they denied appropriations to the District of Columbia, because they hate black people. But they can't say that. Instead, they vote against the appropriation and make life hard for a lot of people here. That's the male model."

Like the other sisters, Emma Chappell believes that women, particularly black women, bring a new dimension to the power table. "I think they bring a sense of responsibility and a sense of stability. They bring sincerity and honesty. You'll find that women—and men will kill me for this—are usually more honest than men. Another way of putting it—I think they bring their feminine sensitivity to the world."

Congresswoman Cardiss Collins (D-Ill.) said that a black woman's image of using power was very different from the rush most power brokers describe: "It seems to me that men think power is moving the mountains, moving the earth. Or at least shaking it up. Black women tend to have a different vision. I think women understand that power is getting the job done, not making a lot of noise, gyrations, doing a lot of talking and what have you. But really getting the job done."

Maxine Waters said precisely the same thing: "I use power to get things done. That means trying things that other people haven't tried. It isn't necessarily confrontational. But you need new ideas."

Reverend Willie Barrow expressed her view of power in terms of public service: "If you really want to be powerful, if you really want to be influential, and if you really want people to support you, then just serve. Remember those two brothers who went to sit at the right hand of God and said, 'I want to be the greatest and if I sit over here I'll be the greatest.' The Lord said, 'Now, if you really want to be great, serve. Help somebody.'

"I am powerful because I am a serving woman. Because of my service, t'aint nobody going to take that power away from me because the people will not allow it. When I deliver, I deliver from my heart."

Most of the black women who ended up in powerful positions said they never sought them. They had long histories of doing whatever job needed doing, and doing it exceptionally well. Dr. Dorothy Harris, president of the National Association of Social Workers, echoed Reverend Barrow's comments by saying that her power came from "serving wherever I was needed in whatever way I could. Giving of myself without regards to price or anything else, just sticking true to my goal and my people, that's been the support system that has raised me to where I am, nothing else but that."

Most Phenomenal women acknowledged that they did have power, whether they had sought it or not. Congresswoman Barbara-Rose Collins (D-Mich.) said it simply came with the job. "I am in the position to influence local, national, and international programs. I am in a power position and you must separate that from personal power."

Josephine D. Davis, on leave from the presidency of York College CUNY, agreed, but again pointed out the difference between male and female perceptions of power. "As black women, we're shaping our own image of power. I have a reluctance to say I have power, but not a reluctance to use it. Power basically comes with the position."

Others expressed a more philosophical viewpoint. Maxine Waters believes that everyone has power: "Some of us tap into it and understand how to use it. And we are not afraid to use it. Others take longer to discover their power, or they assign their power to other people."

The theory that power always corrupts, and sometimes corrupts absolutely, is the best available argument for making the transference and redistribution of power an ongoing process. This might suggest that black women are uniquely qualified for real political power in good part because they have had so little of it.

They are the last to arrive at the power table, bringing with them a profound experience of discrimination and denial. Congresswoman Carrie P. Meek (D-Fla.), born and reared in Florida during the twilight of de jure segregation, never expected to wind up in Congress. She served twelve years as a Florida state legislator before making the leap to the federal level. At the age of sixty-six, Carrie Meek arrived in Congress when most women are back home rocking their grandchildren. For her, the lateness of the hour serves a purpose: "The ten black women in Congress have a cohesiveness that comes from knowing that we were the last to get here. We have a tougher road to follow, more problems to solve. So we have to get about the business of getting it done."

Black women take their seats with a different understanding, an alternative worldview, and a new vision. They are not there to step into the existing shoes of the power elite. They are there to crack the mold. Their definition of power is inescapably tied to their agendas.

"Our mission has been clearly defined for us," Carrie Meek said. "That is, we must help our people. I have tunnel vision when it comes to that. As a black woman, I must remember the history that is behind me."

Congresswoman Corrine Brown (D-Fla.) wrapped it up: "Power is the ability to get things done, to make things better for the people."

The ability to "make things better for the people" was the primary motivation of all of the black women now serving in Congress, and the same theme resonated in the testimony of all of the Phenomenal women interviewed for this book, regardless of where they were working. When it comes to their intentions, regardless of their sphere of influence, they speak with one voice. Does that mean that Phenomenal women represent only African Americans in their agendas? On the contrary, their agendas join together men and women of all races, creeds, and cultures who are struggling to achieve fairness, equality, and a sense of humanity: "I'm relating to senior citizens, to babies, to youth, to uneducated and educated, to people that live in high-rises and people who live in suburbs. I'm pulling it all together. You need nothing but people."

Black women are aware that when you help people on the bottom, you automatically help everyone else. Their power mandate stems from an understanding of the past and an appreciation of how change comes about. In the past, efforts aimed toward helping the most disadvantaged people in America have usually produced even greater benefits for those already slightly above them. For example, the Freedmen's Bureau was originally established to provide education for those formerly enslaved but offered education and other services to poor whites as well, and ultimately free public education was extended to every child in America. The Fourteenth Amendment, which guarantees the rights of all citizens to due process and equal protection under the law, has most often been used to protect the rights of white Americans. In our time, the Civil Rights Act of 1964, initiated to increase opportunities for African Americans, was extended to include women of every color and ethnic background. It's common knowledge, although seldom discussed, that the greatest number of beneficiaries of affirmative action—from employment in higher education and big business, to integration of police and fire departments, to small-business opportunities—have been white women.

Congresswoman Cynthia McKinney described the black woman's service agenda this way: "We have to work hard to make sure that in everything we do we are trying to prevent the negative impact of politics on people's lives. We also have the power to deliver services to our constituents. Not just congressional services, but that voice, that representation, in all levels of government for people who have been locked out, left behind.

"I celebrate the differences among people. Those differences are what we need to patch together coalitions that work. And not just political coalitions. Sometimes it's an economic coalition, sometimes a social coalition. Celebrating those differences and being part of the difference is a good thing."

Congresswoman Eddie Bernice Johnson (D-Tex.) summed up their thinking: "Eliminate the posturing, dispense with the rhetoric, and be about the business of delivering programs and services that will improve the quality of people's lives."

Sisters are aware that they are constantly at risk of being cut down or co-opted. They know their positions are tenuous and that they must be vigilant at all times. However, the instability does not make them anxious. Unlike leaders who consider themselves autonomous, many sisters believe the source of their power comes from a higher authority.

According to Carrie Meek, "I think I got most of my power from God and then from the people. The fact that they empowered me to come to Congress, the first black person in 129 years from the state of Florida, that gives me power. Every time I go back to my district, they pat me on the shoulder and say, 'We're glad to see you. Keep on doing what you're doing. We're praying for you.' That gives me the power."

Reverend Willie Barrow also said God was the source of her power: "We always took a little and made much. That's why we can take a little knowledge and run the country, take a little food and feed a multitude. We've always taken a little and made much because we always put it in the hands of God."

Paula Banks, president of the Sears Foundation, said, "The power that we have as African American women is the same power we've had through the generations. Our power is that we can stay the course when others don't expect us to. Our power is that we have inner strength that allows us to persevere. Many times we are able to help people do what they don't want to do, without them even knowing that they've been helped. Without them even recognizing that there is a power behind them that has propelled them forward to do something, that if you took the frontal attack, they would never do it."

For Phenomenal black women power seems to be a combination of understanding history, being moved by the power of the spirit, and hearing the cries of an oppressed people. They are motivated by their social consciousness and epic memories. They view power in the collective sense.

Black women of enormous power are frequently portrayed as brash, brazen loudmouths loaded with attitude and righteous indignation. This image is not accidental. Sisters are clear that they are in their jobs in order to make changes, not to maintain the status quo. They deliberately avoid doing business "the old-fashioned way." Justice Leah Sears-Collins of the Georgia supreme court believes that black women with power should have attitude. "We're freer because there are no role models. You can do your own thing. Create your own models. And we have a broad range to work with. We've got more variety, more character, and more breathing room—and we damn well take it."

Maxine Waters is seldom surprised when her congressional colleagues and staff comment on her style. "I've heard it said many times that the people around here are 'so afraid of you.' I don't know what that means. All that I can think of is that they are accustomed to people of lesser status knowing their place. They're accustomed to their wives knowing their place. They're accustomed to women they have come in contact with generally knowing their place. To encounter a free black woman who does not know her place must be frightening."

In fact, none of the Phenomenal women were consistently brash. And some were notably smooth, polished, and soft-spoken—most of the time.

Paula Banks observed that all were capable of pulling the stops out when they needed to. "The African American women that I know have a quiet but effective presence; if needed, they can be as dogmatic and loud and vociferous as the next person. They are very bright, they are well read, they are well versed, they are loving, they are caring, they have a class about them, a dignity about them. And they have the ability to manage an inordinate amount of professional and personal stress with class and grace that is second to none."

As far as personal appearance goes, sisters display a varied stylishness that often confounds their opponents. While they obviously look different from their white counterparts, they also look different and behave differently from one another. You cannot pigeonhole sisters according to personal appearance, patterns of speech, or the manner in which they present their arguments.

Congresswoman Cynthia McKinney wears her hair in distinctive braids. "People tell me I need to have chemicals in my hair if I want to look congressional and if I want to represent both black and white people. I don't care about the straightness of my hair, and I hope my constituents don't care either. They ought to care about where I stand on the issues and what I bring to the table when I sit down to make policy.

"I may not subscribe to the norm, as far as behaving or looking the way leadership is supposed to look. But by not suppressing those things about me that make me different—by acknowledging that difference and, in some cases, even accentuating it—that's leadership."

Roberta Palm Bradley of Pacific Gas & Electric agreed: "I don't want to be one of the boys. The role I play is that I am diversity, diversity of thought. I certainly *look* different than they do. Out of diversity, organizations become stronger. I'm the one who can ask those questions that our customers would ask, or our employees would ask. I think that's the great value that I bring. I really don't try to be one of the boys."

For these sisters, leadership was more important than power, although the words themselves are often used interchangeably by many people. Through trial and error, their leadership model developed, and with little or no communication between themselves, they all conceived of a remarkably similar way of doing business. Their new leadership model is creative, it's black, and it's female.

Strong-arm tactics do not usually play a part in the equation. Carrie Meek's approach to leadership was typical: "I am willing to confront people, but not in a scorch-and-burn sort of way. If it involves solving the particular problems of the black community, I'll confront them."

Doing their own homework and carefully laying the groundwork was a consistent theme among the sisters. Mary Hatwood Futrell: "I do my own background work. I am not comfortable with someone coming in and simply briefing me. I want to go through all of it."

When interviewed, Shirley Franklin was, as chief manager of the city of Atlanta, responsible for the development of all city government departments and seven thousand city employees, who reported to nine different commissioners. Her city budget was $1 billion, in five different funds. When it came to finding solutions to problems, she did her own homework. When interviewed, she explained: "Sometimes I don't have time to do all of the research I like to do because the decision has to be made quickly. But I tend to be the kind of person who still goes to the library and does the homework. Or I'm calling a commissioner or three commissioners for information. I use them like a stack of books. I don't presume to know all that they know. I want their best thinking, and then I want them to answer my questions. I draw conclusions based on what I know about everything around me. Then I try to determine if the idea is saleable—based on what I know about the politics, the personalities, the resources available in the environment."

They have translated all of this into a new way of doing business. Instead of controlling from the top, these sisters were adept at establishing relationships and building support systems from the bottom up *and* from the top down, frequently switching hats from powerful head honcho to soothing mother figure. They could engage fully in this process without relinquishing their authority.

The Sister Power leadership model is missing the ego thing and the know-it-all thing. In their place is a greater openness to listen to new ideas. As they travel this new road, they are willing to ask for directions. Carrie Meek: "I lead by trying to get in where the group is working, offer my services, if needed. If not needed, I'm willing to follow."

Marcia Gillespie consciously worked to eliminate the hidden hierarchy among her staff. "We meet, talk, discuss, and argue to come to conclusions about things. My basic belief is that we are all leaders and we are all followers. It depends on the moment, the hour, and the circumstances."

Emma Chappell said she made a point to include others in the decision-making process. "Oftentimes I see where I can do something just as well myself, but having grown up in the banking industry I realize we very seldom do anything that we don't talk to other colleagues about. For best results, I tend to share information with people and also seek information from them. Ultimately, I make a decision and live by it."

Shirley Franklin gave a vivid example of the potential benefits of leading by participatory democracy. "We had some people die about five years ago in a bad ice storm because they froze to death. The next day, two women from my office staff came in and said they thought we needed to do something about that. I gave them twenty-four hours to come up with an idea, and now we have one of the most aggressive shelter programs in the country."

Marcia Gillespie believes she derives her leadership style from her heritage: "I come from talkative people, you know, talking in terms of how black folks do and women folks do. The importance of talking is something that I am clear about. Maybe growing up where I did, it is a kitchen table style where we can sit around that table and talk about stuff. Goodness knows what is going to come out of it, but usually something good happens."

Marcia said that much of her understanding of what to do with power resulted "from time spent in the river." "I think I have become more patient. I have become more thoughtful, I hope."

Into the mix of participatory democracy, sisters added yet another distinctive word: *vision*.

Roberta Palm Bradley said she was always thinking about what the future might bring: "I look outward. I don't spend a whole lot of time in the present. I spend my time in the future, trying to guess what it will bring. Then I try to make changes now to help in the future. I see myself as a visionary, and I have a visionary leadership style.

"I feel it is my responsibility to set the overall direction of the organization I lead. You look to the future, and make your best guess based on the information you have and the education that you've gained. You try to develop a focus and a common direction for your organization."

Mary Hatwood Futrell added the need to persuade others to move toward your vision: "You have to have vision. And you also have to be a strong advocate. You have to be articulate. You have to know the issues, so when you stand up people will respect who you are and respect what you are saying and who you represent. You also have to motivate people and get people to do things. Leadership must be persuasive.

"A leader has to be able to identify and pick people to walk with her, not just those who agree with her, but also those who don't agree, and get people to work together. My leadership style is bringing people together, being a strong advocate, pitching in and helping out. I put in long hours. I have a great sense of pride. I am the kind of leader who is very demanding, not only of others, but of myself as well."

Pamela Carter said she also made a point of articulating her vision to her support staff, as well as organizations and various groups: "I am willing to spend time processing the vision in a way that brings people along. I'm very comfortable working with groups, the larger they are the more comfortable I am. I have definite ideas and I expect people to go in that direction. I give them everything they need to do that and do it well. I focus a great deal of time and effort on the process."

Spending time on "the process" is part of their belief that when subordinates understand what they're doing and why they are doing it, they are motivated to maximum performance. Black women leaders like to surround themselves with highly competent people.

Emma Chappell said, "While you may be ever so smart, it is advisable to surround yourself with qualified people. That's what I do. And whoever I'm working with I advise them to do the same."

They also want their people to excel and move ahead. They believe in putting time and effort into helping their staff develop themselves and their careers. Paula Banks invests in these relationships: "Anyone who thinks that they are a leader must take the opportunity to mentor and be mentored. Those who do not take the opportunity to grow and help others to grow cannot be called leaders. They have not decided to take the path."

None of this means that these sisters are soft. On the contrary, flexibility seems to add to their muscle. As their opponents well know, these sisters enjoy playing hardball. Nor does "helping others grow" mean that they are mother hens. Mentoring takes some unusual twists in the hands of sisters.

Dorothy Brunson, CEO of Brunson Communications Inc., sees every negative encounter with an employee as an opportunity to encourage that individual's growth. "I have fired people. I will let anybody go. I don't care who it is. But I will not let anybody go without giving them a personal firing. I never fire people ad hoc. I always say, 'Let's talk about what you do have going, and let me help steer you. Get your act together.' I've done that for hundreds and hundreds, gotten them back on track.

"I remember one woman who had spent five years trying to be a disc jockey. She couldn't even speak English. I taped her one day and said, 'Not only do you crackle and squeak, you don't even make clear sentences. Do me a favor, go take a journalism course.' She went back to school and became a top-notch journalist. That happens all the time. I try not to be emotional with people. I do my best to be honest.

"I do this with everybody. I mean literally. If I am on the street and a bum says something to me, I say, 'What is wrong with you? Tell me what is wrong with you that you are lying on the street. What is it that you need?' I am always doing that. One man said to me, 'I'm not asking you for anything, because you always want to know how come I'm not working.' But you know, someone can always ask me for money."

A final common thread distinguishes the black female leadership model. Roberta Palm Bradley emphasized that effecting change usually meant breaking the existing rules. "You certainly cannot be an African American woman in this society without thinking, hoping, that the future will be better. Part of my leadership style is that I welcome a lot of breaking of the rules. I've been called controversial because of that. But I really do believe that if you don't question why you do things, then you're not doing your job. You continually have to ask yourself, 'Why am I doing this? What kind of value does it have?' "

Mary Hatwood Futrell, whose post as president of the National Education Association demanded sensitive diplomacy, believes it is essential to take risks: "I know that if I say or do the wrong thing it could cause a lot of problems, but you have to take the risk. You have to try new things and not really know how they are going to turn out."

A final word on this came from Cynthia McKinney: "The model is: Don't listen to the people who think they know. Don't let them tell you what they think they know, because ultimately, you know better. That's my model!"

When Aretha Franklin sings "I wanna be a do-right woman," the spirit of her voice captures the intensity and emotional commitment felt by all Phenomenal women. They are "do-right women" who strive continuously to do the right thing in the larger community. They want to involve more people in worthy projects, to be sensitive to their needs, and to invest themselves in human relationships.

Their leadership model does not exist in a vacuum. They are trying to fulfill a mandate that includes all forgotten Americans and global citizens. Sisters are using their model to alter the distribution of resources; to implement new services and programs; and to challenge stereotypical images regarding the potential of blacks and women. They have set a place at the table for those whose voices are seldom heard.

In their hands, Sister Power is defined as the collective spirit of culturally conscious black women committed to principled leadership. These women never lose sight of the fundamental need for social change. They carry their commitment into local neighborhoods, small towns, and big cities, and into the citadels of business and government.

Through politics, business, education, housing, endowments, voting rights, crime prevention, and community action, they are finding creative solutions to stubborn, seemingly insurmountable social problems. Black women have earned their positions at the nation's power tables, and for them it is the culmination of years of preparation combined with a conscious decision to accept the responsibility of leadership. In an ironic twist of fate, those once totally denied are now providing direction for a new generation of Americans.

11

Coming Full Circle: Messages to Our Sisters

In the winter of my life I want to be able to sit down and talk with young women and tell them how to make it and how I made it. I want to talk about how we got over. It is not easy. You have to be tough skinned. Can't cry a lot. I don't believe in crying. You've got to be tough, but not trying to act like a man, because I want to keep my femininity. I love being a woman.

I say all the time, 'A female I was born, a child I grew up to be, a wife I try to be, a mother I'm proud to be, a Christian I chose to be, a minister I was called to be, and black I must be.' With all of them *be*'s going for me, I can be anything I'm big enough to be."

—*Reverend Willie Barrow*
Chairman and CEO, Operation PUSH

Gwendolyn Calvert Baker was nine years old when she stood waiting with other girls on the steps of the local YWCA for the grand opening of the brand-new community swimming pool—but she was not allowed to enter. "When I was interviewed for the job as director of the YWCA, USA, I thought, 'My gosh, they've come full circle, and so have I. Here I am being asked to consider being CEO of an organization that at one time refused my entry.' Isn't that strange, all that happens."

The "strangeness" that guided Gwendolyn to the executive post of the YWCA, with 1.1 million members and a $50 million budget, was part of a rippling force that continues to alter the gender and complexion of the faces of power in many areas.

For Pamela Carter, winning the office of state attorney general was her greatest professional achievement to date. Pamela carried into the position the memories of all of the black men and women denied equal justice under the law. But more specifically, she carried the memories of her grandfather, a black lawyer trained in the twenties who was denied his right to practice law in the state of Indiana because of his race. "As I look back and as I look forward, I realize what it entailed. This was monumental." That Pamela's grandfather managed to pass on his love for the law to her, that she would pursue her own legal career with vigor despite such painful discrimination and one day become the ultimate legal authority in the very state that denied him access was truly "monumental." All of the ancestors are celebrating.

As the reputations of these Phenomenal women grow, they receive constant requests from various community and national groups to elicit their support and involvement. Emma Chappell, president of United Bank of Philadelphia, said, "The demands of the community are large, from both blacks and women. Both look to me for advice, for contacts, for networks, and for help. They need me to be a good role model. If nothing else motivates you, you want to excel because you realize how much you influence other people. I want to do the very best that I can."

They are spread very thin. In addition to their professional positions, all are serving on the boards of national and local corporations, college boards, and social and community agencies.

They are serving, and serving until it hurts, in jobs that are never finished. Fran Farmer, former president of Operation Crossroads Africa, whose constant traveling from continent to continent causes many moments of sheer exhaustion, said: "I know a lot of sisters who have done a lot of things, and when one job is done, they just keep on pushing, on to the next thing." The sisters said the strongest power they had was the ability to just keep walking.

C. Delores Tucker described it this way: "So many people are calling on me to do so many things; I do the best I can. People don't know that there are so many fronts for us to work on. They want to see you every hour, at every event, but there are so few of us out there on the national circuit, and the demands are tremendous."

Perhaps the greatest joy Phenomenal women derive from their positions is showing other black women the way to the top. Pamela Carter said: "One reason I sit here talking to you today is to share this story with other sisters." Every Phenomenal woman I interviewed virtually repeated the same phrase. These sisters have arrived, and they intend to bring others along with them.

They are consciously and tirelessly setting about the task of expanding their numbers and picking their own replacements. They are united in this goal: Though they may be the first, they don't want to be the last.

Paula Banks said, "I know that I'm a work in progress. It is not clear yet where the process is to end. I want to stand up in front of a group and look out at the audience and see people like me. As leaders, it is our responsibility to make this wish come true. I want young African Americans to know that as tough as it is out there, as racially segregated and prejudiced as our society still is, with lots of faith and hard work we can still make progress. People are there who are willing to encourage and guide you. I want that to be my legacy."

The older Phenomenal women are imbued with wisdom gathered from years of work in the trenches; their sagacity is matched by the youthful exuberance of sisters who were pushed forward by a changing social climate. Here are their messages, on the job and off:

Pamela Carter said that getting to the top was in some ways easier than it appears, and in other ways more difficult. "First, do the job and do it well. The one thing I always try to do is be very effective in whatever job I do, at whatever point. Know your place—not a racial or social place—but understand your place in the organizational setting. Many people make mistakes by trying to be bigger than they are, or less than they are. Be what you are and do it effectively. Then you'll be recognized, particularly these days when everyone has to pull their own oar in order to help us survive in a global economy. The facts of the situation demand it."

Dorothy Brunson echoed the advice to do the best possible job at all times and in all situations: "I was always the first black woman in the company. I had a keen sense that if I did my job well and found a way to make things better, they would have to deal with me. I can remember being a receptionist. Whereas other receptionists would just chat on the phone, I would ask, 'Do you have more work to do? Can I help you?' As a result, every job I have ever been on, I got promoted or I got a write-up, or the bosses immediately said, 'She can type well, she can do this well, she can do that well.' Some of the other employees may have been reluctant about me, but I always found a nice way to get on the boss's side."

Roberta Palm Bradley concurred: "To my young sisters I would say, Take advantage of every opportunity. No assignment is beneath you. Take that assignment and make yourself shine like a star. Remain upbeat and positive. Don't allow yourself to slip into the negative. Stop searching for the boogie man. For every door that is closed, find a window of opportunity. It means working very hard, and sometimes working at things you really don't want to do. Keep the past and present in perspective, but always keep your eyes to the future."

Emma Chappell emphasized the importance of a thorough education and also recommended making sure that sisters find ways to enjoy life: "I don't mean trying drugs and I don't mean sex. I mean just plain enjoying life. Establish a life with your family, positive communication with one another. If need be 'Go back to the stoop' to rejuvenate the body, spirit, and soul."

Pamela Carter also included personal life on her list of priorities: "And if you have a family, never neglect that. That's going to be the thing that sustains you. The rest will come and go. But your family won't. It's too tough an environment to withstand if you don't feel good about yourself and if your family is not there to help you out. Your self-esteem—if you're a little shaky on that, work on it in some context, because it will hurt you if you don't. Even if you need to meet with people like us. Or to have lunch with a variety of individuals so you can have positive rays sent your way. So you know you have more going for you than you think."

Reverend Willie Barrow had some practical sisterly advice about personal time that all women in power have had to learn. "Budget some time for yourself to keep looking good because in your career there are certain expectations. You can have any style you want, but you have to look good. If you have no money, your clothes still have to look good, even if you have to wash them and iron them every night. Your hair has to be right, meaning it has to be clean and look nice. Your face has to be right, your nails have to be done, you have to be smelling good, and you have to keep thin. You have to take time for these things."

Marcia Gillespie has many opportunities to speak to young women, and she always starts with the same message about developing individuality: "Don't struggle trying to do me. You have to be able to do yourself. Have your own style. You can do it. It ain't no mystery. It doesn't take a rocket scientist. What we do is about some logic, about some mother wit, or, as my Nanna would say, 'You gotta have people skills.' "

She reinforced the importance of education and added the need for awareness of national and global issues. "It's rough out there. You gotta be able to learn how to rock and roll. Men, jobs, our relationship to the world. The nature of the conversation has changed. The discussion has broadened. The kitchen table is bigger. National and global issues are topics of discussion. The lessons to be learned are essentially the same, and you can set your own priorities. There is a role for us in the women's movement, the black movement, environmental movement, and all the submovements."

Marcia points out the similarities between the lives of young black women and the lives of their mothers and grandmothers. "We have to be a lot of things as black women. This is not a burden. Nor does it mean that you must follow everyone who tells you to 'jump, jump' to prove how black you are. We do need to nurture the warrior spirit in sisters. We don't have time to be nice girls—and what the hell is a nice girl? We do need 'bad' black women. And we need to encourage young sisters to be as bad as they can be."

When it came to developing and maintaining individuality, Fran Farmer pulled no punches: "I would say, Gather around you some resources that are yours, no matter where you go. I would say, Don't concede an inch. Don't ever let somebody rip at your vital sense of self. People can fight with you or disagree. They will criticize you. They will take issue. That's fine. But whatever they say about you, there is a part of you that you must keep vibrant and strong and proud. A part that says, 'F—— 'em, I don't care.' "

Dorothy Brunson gave some thought to the idea of maintaining cultural identity in the mainstream business world: "I wouldn't describe myself as a race woman today. I don't have to say it that hard anymore. I am very comfortable in every environment. I am very clear about being black. I am very clear that I have to keep before other people a certain new reality as it relates to black people. I can just be me, and then, from time to time, pull out certain things that need to happen. So, yes, in the new sense, I have no problem with being a race woman. I love it."

And an inspiring word from Maxine Waters: "You cannot be afraid to say what you feel and think. Examine yourself and examine what you care about. Try to understand *why* you care. Or why something bothers you a lot. This kind of self-development is important. This is what allows you to be in the middle of madness, and come out whole.

"If you're going to be in racist situations, or any difficult or highly competitive situations, you've got to get rid of fear. You've got to be able to say, 'This is the bottom line. This is the point you can't go beyond with me.' If you don't develop that, you'll end up feeling bad about yourself, uncertain. If you yourself don't know what the boundaries are, you start to feel like a dog when you go home. If you continue that way, it will eat you up and make you feel like a lesser person. You can't be the person you could be.

"You have to deal with self, and the truth about who you are and what you do. If you've got things about yourself that you don't feel good about, you've got to deal with them. Deal with these things first, before you really get out there, so you don't get whipped."

Among the inspirational messages, the sisters also had some words of caution. All emphasized the need to remember the past, and several voiced their concern that the younger generation might be losing their sense of heritage.

Paula Banks believes that some young African Americans are unaware of just how dangerous and difficult the road to opportunity has been. "There were times when I didn't know if I could pay for coffee. Some young African Americans have no realization or appreciation of that. Those now in their thirties are beginning to have arrogance.

"I'm not talking about those who are struggling inside our cities with poverty. I'm talking about those we've helped to bring along. We have protected them. We've made it so glorious and so wonderful—they have their cars, their insurance is paid, their tuition is paid, they wear their designer clothes. Instead of teaching them 'To those that a lot has been given, a lot is expected,' we've helped them to grow up believing 'To those that a lot has been given, a lot more should be given'! They seem unaware that only a few generations ago they were picking cotton! You sit there thinking, 'I'm old. What have we done? What has gone wrong? How can we undo it?'

"So, in building this network of young African Americans we have to make sure they understand what is really important. We must speak of our values. We must teach our young people to value one another, value the sanctity of life, and to give back. Those are the things that gave us the foundation from which we were able to grow."

Mary Hatwood Futrell, who is so closely in touch with young people all over the country, also recognized the hazardous trend. "One of the things that really scares me is that so many young people coming along take what we have for granted; they don't understand the sense of history behind how long and how bitter that struggle was. They seem unaware that people died for us to be able to do the things that we are doing today."

Congresswoman Barbara-Rose Collins voiced her concern about the lack of perception among even well-educated black youth: "We have a whole generation of children who know nothing about the Civil Rights movement. Know nothing of Martin Luther King Jr. or Malcolm X. They're rediscovering them now, but they knew nothing and thought, as I did as a ten-year-old child, that life was hunky-dory. I have had young thirty-year-old black M.B.A.'s and C.P.A.'s tell me, 'I'm apolitical.' I say, 'What the hell do you mean, you're apolitical? How do you think you got your job?' "

Cynthia McKinney is consciously making an effort to pass the lessons of the past on to her eight-year-old son. She explains to him the sacrifices they both must make in order for her to serve the people. "I explain to him that somebody has to be responsible for making sure that everybody gets their fair shake in life. Because of the opportunity that I have to serve the public, and to serve him and the needs of children like him, most times I cannot be with him.

"I want him to understand that he doesn't have many choices

in life, either. He has to excel in school. He has to put education first. He has to give back to the community in a meaningful way by becoming a businessman, or becoming a police officer, or by becoming an upstanding, hardworking family man.

"My struggle right now is to teach my son that he is different and that he can play soccer with his little white friends, but they could end up being his boss—not because they're better academically, but because they have advantages that he doesn't have because he starts out two shakes behind. It is so important to me to have him understand that there is nothing more important than excellence. Every day I tell him, 'Nothing less than your best.' If he begins to accept anything less, then he's doomed to second-class positions, or second-class citizenship. That is something that we can fight, we must fight."

Cynthia is undeterred by the present disdain for affirmative action. "We look and see race-based remedies being chipped away, and we must tell our young people that there's nothing less than being the top in terms of qualifications. That's the only thing that is acceptable. Otherwise, we could slip back into a serious state of disrepair as a people, as we are doing. When we look and see that the institutions have failed our young people—those same young people are now failing society and are now failing black people. We must instill in them, whether the institutions are the best or not, that they have to have the best within themselves."

When it comes to bringing up the next generation to fill their shoes, Unita Blackwell wastes no time feeling sorry for their predicaments or sympathizing with their problems. "I am the type that says, 'Get up. Get on here. You can do it.' Like people did for me. None of us had professions. Dorothy Height used to tell us, 'All of us are professionals in this room. Because you all are organizing people.' That's what I try to do for young people. Give meaning to what they are doing, tell them that it has a name. It has an answer. I remember one woman older than me who said, 'I went home after hearing you speak, and I said, "I can do that."' And she did. She became a mayor in South Carolina.

"I just want you to know that we poor have been exploited. And now it looks like we are being more exploited than ever. The most important thing is to get the movement to moving. It is you folks, the young ones, that have to do it your way. Keep moving. We can be the best. I had no idea it was thirty years ago when we started all this. I don't feel that. I don't even feel tired."

Reverend Willie Barrow, a deeply religious woman, often summarized her thoughts in terms of her faith. Her words seem to capture the essence of what Phenomenal women feel. Thus, with the deepest gratitude to all the sisters who so willingly opened their minds and hearts for this book, some final words belong to her:

"God is my secret. Put God first. Create a base. Don't ever operate without an airport, because you can't land. Establish an airport. So when you zoom and climb and climb, always come back to the airport. Land. If you keep that ground, you will go anywhere you want to go in business, politics, labor, in all of your work and all of your aspirations. Nobody can hinder you because that's a power that is greater than books. Greater than political power. Greater than death. With God Power, can't nobody touch you. You can ask for the sky and the stars and get it. Don't worry about money because you're already rich. If you bring to the storehouse your offerings, then God will open up the windows of heaven. I am never broke, never lost for words."

Sister Power is a broad-based movement from the top down and the bottom up. Throughout the country, examples of black women conducting themselves as Phenomenal women in large and small roles are plentiful. That black women could rise in a society that so severely restricted their opportunities is an inspirational American success story. Their strength and fortitude are powerful examples for everyone.

Unlike their Potentiate sisters, Phenomenal women speak proudly of their heritage and faithfully preserve their connections to the African American community. They have the ability to rock with the rhythm and go with the flow, traits so characteristic of the black American experience. The essence of their being—as blacks and as women—is not for sale. Their integrity is not for sale. They are solid as a rock and refuse to be deterred from a just and righteous movement.

The struggle continues, the battle is still raging, the victory not yet won. The truth is that even those sisters who have made it are standing on a tenuous plateau, in constant danger of falling back down the slope. As we approach the twenty-first century, America again is faced with the question of the "color line." This is one hundred years after Du Bois sounded the clarion call about the role that race would play in the future. Added to the unresolved issues of race are a gender line, a justice line, and a truth line. It may well be that we need a new black women's movement, imbued with the spirit, strength, tenacity, and vision similar to the Black Women's Club Movement that unfolded at the turn of the century.

Cynthia McKinney offers a message to all who are concerned about the future of the struggle:

"I wish the black community would give more financial resources to people trying to do the right thing on behalf of the community. It is devastating. I celebrate my freedom up here in Washington. I'm free to vote any way I want, free to say anything I want. All these corporate people come in and they have their agenda to present to me. So I always have my agenda for them. I ask who they do business with by race and by gender. I want to know what their management looks like by race and by gender.

"We have our priorities here, too. I prioritize people by the way they prioritize us. But it's difficult when I have to go back to the same person whom I just finished castigating, and ask for a campaign contribution because my people won't get up off a dime to help people like me who are committed to the struggle. If we are going to control our own destinies, we must fund our own struggle."

Phenomenal women cannot wait for the final march to Zion. To all Americans in search of equal participation and equal opportunity, they say unanimously: "Support us in our efforts to turn this society around. Time is of the essence."

Selected Bibliography

Congressional Record, 1994.

Douglas, Ann. *Terrible Honesty.* New York: Farrar, Straus and Giroux, 1995.

Edwards, Audrey, and Dr. Craig K. Polite. *Children of the Dream: The Psychology of Black Success.* New York: Anchor Books, 1992.

Franklin, John Hope. *From Slavery to Freedom.* New York: Alfred A. Knopf, 1974.

Giddings, Paula. *When and Where I Enter.* New York: Bantam Books, 1984.

Smith, Jessie Carney. *Epic Lives.* Detroit: Visible Ink Press, 1993.

Sweetman, David. *Women Leaders in African History.* Oxford: Heinemann Educational Books, 1984.

Yee, Shirley. *Black Women Abolitionists.* Knoxville: University of Tennessee Press, 1992.

Index